ECCLESIA

I

MATTHEW THE POOR

HIS BODY
THE CHURCH IMMORTAL

FOREWORD
METR. SABA (ISBER)

INTRODUCTION BY
MONK BARNABAS EL MACARI

*EDITION, TRANSLATION FROM ARABIC
AND INTRODUCTION*

*MONKS OF THE MONASTERY
OF ST. MACARIUS*

ST. MACARIUS PRESS
MONASTERY OF SAINT MACARIUS THE GREAT (EGYPT)

ISBN

979-8-9898270-0-8

Library of Congress Control Number

2025933658

Series

Ecclesia

Translation from Arabic and Editing

Monks of the Monastery of St Macarius

Introduction

Monk Barnabas el Macari

Icon on the Cover

George Makary

Cover Design

David Georgy

Format

5" x 8"

Pages

165

Second Revised Reprint—June 2025

TABLE OF CONTENT

Foreword by Metr. Saba (Isber)   7

Introduction   15

Editorial Note   33

Preface by Fr. Matthew the Poor   35

PART ONE:
SHADOW OF THE HEAVENLY THINGS

Chapter One

The Tent in the Wilderness   45

Chapter Two

One Sacrifice: The Prefiguration
of Christ's Sacrifice   57

Chapter Three

From the Tent to the Temple In Jerusalem   67

PART TWO:
THE HEAVENLY THINGS THEMSELVES

Chapter One

The New Temple,
His Holy Body   77

Chapter Two

Members in the
Temple of His body   85

Chapter Three

Church and Time   99

Chapter Four

The Unity of the Church's Body   III

PART THREE:
THE PERSONALITY OF THE CHURCH

Chapter One

The Church's Catholicity   119

Chapter Two

The Church Transcends Suffering   127

Chapter Three

The Church Transcends
Sectarianism   137

Chapter Four

Teaching and Fatherhood
inside the Church   143

Chapter Five

The Church and the Holy Spirit   157

FOREWORD

BY METR. SABA (ISBER)

This is a distinctively Alexandrian book, originating from the spirit of the Coptic Orthodox Church in the 1950s. When the venerable fathers of St. Macarius Monastery honored me with the request to pen a foreword to this book in its English edition, I hesitated. As an Antiochian, I love the Alexandrian School, but I am not accustomed to its extreme allegorism. How could I introduce a book that comes from the heart of this tradition? How could I present a work by an author considered a spiritual father and a great scholar in his church? Father Matthew the Poor was an ascetic, a monk, and a scholar. He pioneered the modern monastic renaissance in the Coptic Orthodox Church. Whoever delves into his biography cannot help but be deeply moved by his profound love for God and for living with Him in amazing asceticism and austerity, amidst the silence and harsh climate of the Egyptian desert.

Father Matthew the Poor initiated a spiritual monastic revival based on both tradition and contemporary sciences. After the mid-twentieth century, he is regarded as one of the most significant figures in rooting a conscious spiritual life in the depths of believers. Tens of thousands of Copts found the sweet water of the "life in Christ" through his guidance, teachings, and books. In this sense, he is perhaps the most important in spreading deep-rootedness in heritage while being open to other churches and the modern world at the same time.

After founding his monastic community and establishing the Monastery of Saint Macarius, Father Matthew devoted himself to the ascetic life, having already adopted regular periods of seclusion before fully embracing asceticism. He combined his spiritual experience with the extensive knowledge he acquired, thus enriching the Coptic library with numerous theological and exegetical books.

My hesitation soon dissipated. Perhaps there is a breath of the Holy Spirit in this request. Is it by coincidence that an Antiochian Orthodox metropolitan is asked to introduce a Coptic doctrinal book, whose author paved a way for unprecedented ecclesiastical encounters? Starting in the 1950s, churches began theological dialogues to discover ways to bridge doctrinal gaps between them. These dialogues prepared the ground for ecclesiastical rapprochement and opened paths for dialogues, but their theological statements remained unofficial and were not adopted or pursued by the churches. Fifteen centuries of estrangement and dispute between the two Orthodox Churches, Eastern and Oriental—as defined today—produced distinct doctrinal, spiritual, liturgical and patristic traditions which the dialogue committees and churches did not work on.

What particularly made me accept the request was an experience from the beginning of my priestly life that left an indelible mark on me. In 1992, I spent an entire week at St. Bishoy Monastery in Wadi al-Natrun, observing monastic life from within the monasteries of the Coptic Church. On Sunday morning, I stood aside in the main church of the monastery, following the proceedings of the Divine Liturgy using the Coptic Euchologion. I was struck by a long confession of faith that they recite publicly before partaking of the Holy Communion. When they reached the part concerning the person of the Lord Jesus Christ, they were reciting almost verbatim from the statement of the Fourth Ecumenical Council. I quote from this confession: "This is the life-giving Flesh which your only-begotten Son, our Lord, God, and Savior Jesus Christ, took from our Lady and Queen of us all, the pure holy Theotokos Mary, and made it one with His divinity, without mingling, without confusion, and without alteration... I believe that His divinity parted not from His humanity for a single moment nor a twinkling of an eye."

Some theologians from both churches may differ on accepting the results of theological dialogue. Father Matthew's uniqueness, though, being firstly a monk and secondly a scholar, lies in his belief that true encounter is brought about by God, not by scholars who may prepare for it, when all meet in Him. With this faith, he adopted the teaching of Saint Dorotheos of Gaza in depicting the circle and the center, considering the radii starting from points on the circumference toward the center as an image of each believer's path in their journey to God. As the radii approach the center, they draw closer to one another until they unite in God, who makes them one in Him.

Suppose we were to take a compass, insert the point, and draw the outline of a circle. The center point is the same distance from any point on the circumference. Now concentrate your minds on what is to be said! Let us suppose that this circle is the world and that God himself is the center; the straight lines drawn from the circumference to the center are the lives of men. To the degree that the saints enter into the things of the spirit, they desire to come near to God; and in proportion to their progress in the things of the spirit, they do in fact come close to God and to their neighbor. The closer they are to God, the closer they become to one another; and the closer they are to one another, the closer they become to God.

The theological dialogues between the two churches (Eastern and Oriental) focused on the fundamental faith issue: the person of Christ. However, the theological, liturgical, and patristic heritage that accumulated over fifteen centuries after the schism remained untouched until Father Matthew paved the way to it in his book, or rather his most precious and widely distributed encyclopedia, "Orthodox Prayer Life." After each chapter discussing an aspect of prayer, he arranged a collection of sayings of the holy Fathers of the Church, including those of the Eastern Orthodox Church. For the first time in modernity, a Coptic book cited the teachings of saints who lived in the centuries following the schism of 451, after the Council of Chalcedon. This book spread throughout all the churches of the Middle East and introduced the Christians to the spirituality of the Coptic Church in an unprecedented way. To indicate the importance of the path of spiritual life in reaching a confluence among churches, we quote Father George Khodr's letter to Father Matthew at that time. In his letter, he said: "For the first time, the Greeks are being taught by a Coptic book."

In my opinion, this is the most significant work Father Matthew penned. He presented the believers of his church with spiritual teachings from modern Orthodox saints who were neither familiar nor known in his church, but rather considered as heretics. To frequently cite saints like Saint Theophan the Recluse (†1894) and Saint John of Kronstadt (†1909), and even Saint Gregory Palamas (†1395) and others, meant entering into forbidden territory at that time. This step required great courage and cost him dearly. Nevertheless, he paved the way and bridged the long spiritual gap with his spiritual experience. This laid the foundation for an openness and a spiritual encounter between the Eastern Orthodox and Coptic churches, starting in the Arabic-speaking world and later extending to the Greek and Slavic worlds.

He opened paths for rapprochement between the two churches, which, if supported as it should have been, would have seen significant progress on the ground based on the shared faith and the common spirituality. Father Matthew's uniqueness lay in reminding those working in the ecumenical field that Christian rapprochement is based on the common faith, provided that everyone meets in God, by following the holy and authentic path of the Church's saints.

As for this book, "The Immortal Church," it is one of the earliest writings of Father Matthew, with its first Arabic edition published in 1959, during a period when the author was living in profound asceticism in a barren desert spot with only salty water available.

Father Matthew addresses the subject of the Church based on the Holy Scriptures, following the allegorical-spiritual interpretation that has distinguished the Alexandrian theological school throughout Christian history. What is noteworthy in this book is that it relies solely on what is mentioned in the Holy Scriptures about the Church, without being enriched by the teachings of the Fathers, as he did in the previously mentioned book. There is no doubt that the reason is that he wrote it during a period when he was living a very harsh ascetic life. At that time, he lived in an isolated part of the Egyptian desert, accompanied only by the Holy Scriptures and a few brothers who had become monks with him.

The book explores the dimensions of the Church, according to the author, considering her as one, holy, catholic, and apostolic. I recommend reading it slowly, as the Coptic style of writing and expression might seem difficult to Western readers due to its unfamiliarity. Father Matthew traces the foundations of the Church back to the Old Testament to reveal its hidden image there and then gradually unveils this image until he reaches the New Testament, where everything is revealed with the incarnation of the second person of the Holy Trinity and the commencement of His salvific economy.

In his writing journey, the author delineates three successive paths. He titles the first part "The Shadows of Heavenly Things," where he meticulously reveals the images known in biblical studies as prototypes, which symbolize the yet-to-be-revealed realities. In this presentation, Father Matthew follows the traditional Christian method of reading the Old Testament, faithfully adhering to the way Christ read the Old Testament in the light of Himself, as He did when handed the scroll of Isaiah in the Nazareth synagogue (cf. Luke 4:16-30). Thus, he taught us to read the Old Testament in the light of Christ, the New Testament.

The second part has been titled "The Heavenly Things Themselves," wherein he reveals the face of the Church as clarified in the New Testament. The matter is no longer allegorical or preparatory for what is to come; Christ has come, the veils have been lifted, and we are fulfilling and realizing the promise.

The third part is titled "The Personality of the Church," where he discusses the mission of the Church in the present time. The reader may sense much of the Copts and Egypt's reality in the background of Father Matthew's writings, as he primarily wrote for the clerics and laypeople of his Church. This indicates his pastoral sense and conviction of the necessity for Christians to live their lives based on the foundations of faith derived from the Holy Scriptures, which the Copts diligently preserve, interpret, and contemplate. It is no surprise, therefore, since the Coptic Church is a biblical Church par excellence.

The spiritual fragrance permeates the book. Father Matthew does not deal with a theoretical theological exegesis but seeks to help the readers live what they read. For instance, in his explanation of the Tabernacle, he emphasizes God's presence within it, conveying to the reader that every soul is a Tabernacle that must be prepared for God's presence. In the chapter on becoming members of the Church, he stresses that we must die with Christ to rise with Him and abide in Him.

The book is rich with biblical exegesis according to the Alexandrian school. While I suggest reading it alongside the Holy Scriptures, I invite the reader to savor the pleasure of contemplating its depths and immersing themselves in its profound meanings.

Metropolitan Saba (Isper)
Archbishop of New York and Metropolitan of the
Antiochian Orthodox Christian Archdiocese of North America

INTRODUCTION

The journey of translating this book began several years ago, initially sparked by our desire to bring Father Matthew the Poor's ecumenical writings to a wider audience. At first, our focus was on translating and presenting his ecumenical writings in one volume in a work to be titled *The Mystery of Unity*. However, as we completed the translation and editing, it became quite clear that introducing the readers to Fr. Matthew's ecclesiology was foundational, as it forms the cornerstone of his ecumenical perspectives. Thus, the need emerged for this present volume, entitled *His Body: The Church Immortal*, which serves as the inaugural work in a new series titled *Ecclesia*, dedicated to exploring various themes concerning the Church. It builds upon a first draft that was completed nearly thirty-five years ago but never saw the light. By revisiting and refining this provisional translation, we aimed to create a version that would do justice to Fr. Matthew's profound insights, ensuring that his teachings are accessible to contemporary Western readers.

Historical Backgrounds

Before delving into the main themes of this book, it is helpful to first provide some historical context to aid the readers to understand the circumstances in which Fr. Matthew penned this work.[1] The book was written in 1959, a

---

[1] For a more detailed account of the life of Father Matthew the

crucial moment in the modern history of the Coptic Church as a new pope, Cyril VI (1959–1971),[2] was elected following more than two years of a vacant see marked by significant unrest and uncertainty within the Church.[3] At that time, the Coptic Church was experiencing a weakened spiritual life, which in return left her theologically fragile. Troubled by these difficult conditions afflicting the Church, which he regarded as his own mother, Fr. Matthew withdrew into a prolonged retreat in a secluded hut near Egypt's north coast. He did not inform his disciples but confided his plan solely to one close spiritual son, Samy Kamel, who later became a priest under the name of Fr. Bishoy Kamel (1931–1979),[4] who would travel daily from Alexandria on his small Vespa scooter to bring him food and supplies. During this spiritual retreat, it is likely that Fr. Matthew wrote not only *The Church Immortal* (this was the original title of this book), but also its second volume which is called *The Pentecost.*

Father Matthew's Style

Father Matthew had a very peculiar approach to spiritual writing. Although he was a great proponent of the writings of the early Church Fathers—he used their writings in many

---

Poor, consult our introduction in Matthew the Poor, *Love Took Flesh* (Wadi al-Natrun: St. Macarius Press, 2022), 20–24.

[2] The Coptic Church has canonized his sainthood on June 20, 2013.

[3] See chs. 6–9 in David Fanous, *A Silent Patriarch: Kyrillos VI (1902–1971), Life and Legacy* (Yonkers, NY: St. Vladimir's Seminary Press, 2019).

[4] The Coptic Church has canonized his sainthood on June 9, 2022.

of his books and always encouraged his spiritual sons to read them—one will not find even a single patristic quotation in this book. This exclusion can possibly be attributed to a couple of reasons. First, as previously mentioned, he was living in a very secluded area during the time he was writing this book, without access to any library that could aid his writing, which meant he had to rely entirely on Scripture along with his prayers, personal reflections, and spiritual insights. Second, Fr. Matthew always sought to discover the truth, first and foremost, directly from Scripture, engaging with the biblical text without any preliminary influence from commentaries or external sources. He believed that immersing himself in Scripture first allowed for a more profound and personal revelation of divine truth, uninterrupted by the interpretations of others. Only after spending sufficient time reflecting on the biblical text and forming his own understanding would he turn to the early Church Fathers and select modern biblical studies, seeking confirmation, clarification, or deeper insight into what had already been revealed to him through his personal encounter with the Word of God. That is the reason why he taught himself Hebrew and *koiné* Greek, enabling him to read Scripture in their original languages. He also encouraged his spiritual sons in the monastery to learn these languages, along with modern ones, so they could understand the literal meaning before turning to commentaries or any other books. It is noteworthy that at the time, Arabic commentaries on the Bible were scarce, making access to biblical scholarship and patristic writings difficult. As a result, those who wished to consult such sources had to learn some Western languages. Fr. Matthew's deep immersion in Scripture, free from external commentaries, not only shaped his distinctive spiritual outlook but also infused his writings with authenticity and originality. His works did not arise from academic discourse alone but were born in his inner room, nourished by prayers, biblical reflections, and his lived experience among his monks and the people whom he met. He sets the tone for this book from the very first chapter, stating:

> We will not present academic research on the rituals, nor a study about the Old Testament. Instead, we seek to underline the solid foundation upon which Christ built His Church, and to present the many facets of the cross. In this way, we will lose none of our rights coming from the sacrifice of Christ.[5]

This approach underscores his unwavering commitment to experiencing and transmitting the spiritual essence of Scripture firsthand, making his writings uniquely heartfelt and deeply rooted in both personal revelation and ecclesial tradition. This personal and experiential approach to Scripture shaped both Fr. Matthew's understanding of the Bible and his writing style. Also, as you read this book, do not expect meticulously organized ideas or precise definitions. Instead, you might find the author posing a question and answering it one way, only to later ask the same question and provide an alternative answer. In many instances, he interrupts his flow of words to lift up his heart to the Lord in a short prayer or a plea for the reader to pray with him. Fr. Matthew was not a graduate of a theological school or seminary, nor did he attend prestigious universities, so he does not adhere to academic writing styles or conventional theological structures, especially in his early years of writing and

---

[5] *Infra*, 64.

teaching. Instead, his approach is rooted in personal spiritual experience, often spontaneous and deeply meditative, allowing the Spirit to guide his words rather than following rigid scholarly methods. He was first and foremost a desert spiritual father, a disciple of the Spirit, teaching what the Spirit revealed to him. He once said: "I prayed, and prayed again saying: 'O Lord, your servant is ignorant! I did not graduate from a theological college or seminary. I haven't read theology nor do I know anything in theology. So You teach me! I am coming to You so You open my heart and teach me.' So He taught me."[6]

When Fr. Matthew discusses the Old Testament's Tent of Meeting in the wilderness, the reader might feel as though the author is describing scenes he has personally witnessed. He uses dynamic language that suggests he was spiritually transported through time, standing before the Ark of the Covenant and walking alongside the Levites who carried it. For Fr. Matthew, the Old Testament was a living text, one that could only be truly understood by immersing oneself in its characters and events. Later in the book, he would stop his flow of words to defend his style of the interpretations by saying:

> The reader may think that we are stretching our interpretation of these rituals, going too far beyond their literal meaning. But on the contrary, although we find ourselves overexerted, we have only touched a few of the things that the ancient Jewish rite keeps hidden for the active seekers, so that they may bring

---

[6] Cf. *Mīlād ibn Allāh wa-ruǧūʿ Ādam wa-ḏurriyyatihi ilā Allāh* ("The Birth of the Son of God and the Returning of Adam and His Offspring to God"); sermon on Nativity, 2001 (catalog number: MM-284).

out of its treasures "things new and old" (Matt. 13:52).[7]

There is another aspect concerning the author's style that is of capital importance to generally understand his writings. Although Fr. Matthew did not always adhere strictly to the exegesis of the Alexandrian Fathers, he was deeply inclined toward reading the Scripture through their allegorical and mystical lens. When Fr. Matthew employs symbolism and allegory in his writings, he is in fact following the tradition of many scriptural writers. For instance, in the Old Testament, Ezekiel uses the allegory of the harlot in chapter sixteen to speak about Israel, while St. Paul, in the New Testament, draws on the allegory of Hagar and Sarah in Galatians, chapter four, to speak about the two covenants.

From all that has been mentioned above, what emerges clearly is Fr. Matthew's brilliance: his remarkable ability to translate his direct, mystical experience of the Scripture into words that deeply resonate with and spiritually impact his readers. While many mystics and saints have lived within the Church throughout history, only a select few have possessed the rare gift of articulating their mystical encounters with the Word of God through written expression.

The Church According to Father Matthew the Poor

This brings us to a central question: how did Fr. Matthew perceive the Church? If you are seeking a single, clear-cut definition, you may not find it here. Rather, Fr. Matthew approaches the Church as a mystery that resists rigid definitions, inviting us instead into a deeper contemplation of her reality. Fr. Matthew had a profound love for the Church,

---

[7] *Infra*, 68.

and his heart was always deeply attached to her. He frequently mentioned the Church in his homilies, books, and even in private conversations. The Church was incredibly dear to him. It might seem unusual for a monk and a desert father like him to be so preoccupied with the reality of the Church, given his physical distance from her and the assumption that, because of that, he would be unbothered by her conditions. He was much like St. Anthony the Great: though he lived in the wilderness, he remained deeply attuned to the life of the Church. When the Church needed him, he journeyed twice to Alexandria: once to support the believers during persecution and again during the Arian controversy to defend the faith.[8] The primary motivation behind writing this book was Fr. Matthew's deep concern for the Church's fragile condition and his desire to draw attention to her scriptural, experiential, and doctrinal foundations. It is as if he silently cries out: *The Church is Christ's very Body—how, then, can she be weak?*

The Church's Weakness

Another underlying theme related to the Church's earthly weakness—though not explicitly stated but felt throughout the book—is the idea that the earthly Church is "dark, but lovely" (Song of Sol. 1:5). Though she may appear from the outside flawed, unattractive, or even spiritually and theologically troubled, she remains deeply cherished, revered, and beloved in Fr. Matthew's eyes. He remained steadfast in his

---

[8] See chs. 46 and 69 in St. Athanasius, *The Life of Saint Antony*, Ancient Christian Writers, tr. by Robert T. Meyer, Vol. 10 (New York, NY / Mahwah, NJ: Newman Press, 1978), 59, 78.

devotion to her, even in the face of challenges and opposition from her leaders. To Fr. Matthew, the Church is his mother—imperfect yet beloved—and he considers himself an inseparable part of her. This feeling, akin to constant prayer in his heart, characterized Fr. Matthew's life. Even when he sometimes critiqued her present weaknesses, his love for the Church never wavered or ceased. He beautifully expresses this idea, by saying:

> Even if our body appears to be at odds with the meekness and stillness of the Spirit inside us, as well as the beauty of our soul that is endowed with the righteous acts of the saints, this does not hinder us, because the rough skins of badgers, goats, and sheep were also mismatched with the blue silk underneath them.[9]

Suffering as a Path to Glory

We now turn to another central theme of this book—suffering. Fr. Matthew elevates this concept; consistently unveiling the hidden blessings within passing through suffering that we might easily overlook. He challenges the readers to view suffering not as a burden, but as a passport to glory. He emphatically states:

> Suffering was the ultimate goal of the Incarnation (cf. John 18:11) and the primary goal for which the Son of God descended was to fulfil it.[10]

For Fr. Matthew, suffering is an inseparable part of the Church's identity. From the very first pages of this book, it is

---

[9] *Infra*, 57.
[10] *Infra*, 41.

as if he prepares the Church to bear her cross of suffering and accept it joyfully without grumbling. It is not merely a phase in her life but an ongoing process throughout her earthly existence. Fr. Matthew invites every Church or even any believer inside the Church to embrace suffering and make it a companion, integrating it as part of their own being or as a central aspect of their personality. When he speaks of suffering, he does so with depth and authenticity, coming from experience, not empty words. Although he had only been a monk for eleven years at the time of writing this book, he had already faced many trials and sufferings. He would encounter even more throughout his life— illnesses, persecution from his peers, superiors, Church hierarchies, and even from his own spiritual sons. His life was marked by the Cross in every aspect. He urges that every Church not to shy away from suffering. He uses the words "suffering" and "cross" interchangeably because they represent the same ultimate truth and both will lead to glory and resurrection. When Fr. Matthew speaks of suffering, he draws deeply from the history and the heritage of the Coptic Church—a Church marked by suffering, persecution, and martyrdom. He views this history not just as a memory of the past but as an essential part of the Church's identity. He believes that embracing suffering is vital to living out the true calling of the Church, reflecting the resilience and faith that have defined her for centuries and still until now. He eloquently states:

> Suffering is a testimony. It represents for the Church what it is for Christ as it reveals the mystery of life hidden behind the cross and bears witness to love and sacrifice. It is not possible to proclaim the Christian life if we hide from suffering because

suffering, as we said, is an attribute of the living, not the dead.[11]

The Church Transcends Time and Space

Another essential aspect of his ecclesiology is the Church's transcendence over time and space. Just as he sees suffering as an intrinsic part of the Church's journey, he also perceives the Church as a reality that is not bound by the limitations of the temporal world. Fr. Matthew's mystical perspective reveals that within the Church, space and time take on an entirely new dimension. They are not merely linear progressions of moments but profound spiritual realities that intertwine with eternity. This transcendent quality of the Church flows from Christ's redemptive work, elevating her beyond the constraints of time and space. He articulates this concept as follows:

> Space and time cannot confine the Church. She exists on earth and in heaven, in the present and from the beginning of creation, because Christ's redemptive work reaches back through the ages by virtue of His eternal Spirit, and saves all those who have embraced His promises.[12]

On another occasion, he attributes the Church's timeless transcendence to the work of the Holy Spirit, stating that: "The Church extends into the past and future, just as it is in the present, because the work of the Holy Spirit is boundless."[13] And on the Church's transcendence beyond space, he inquires:

---

[11] *Infra*, 133.
[12] *Infra*, 103.
[13] *Infra*, 103.

Can a limited place contain, within its walls, unlimited souls? We know, in fact, that space is determined by matter. How then can the spirit be confined to a limited place? The place can only hold bodies. As for the believing souls, they do not gather except in the great unlimited Spirit.[14]

The Church and the Parousia

A recurring and central theme in Fr. Matthew's writings—one that also permeates the present book as well—is the Church's role in the *parousia*, the coming of Christ. To better understand this concept and Fr. Matthew's perspective, we will turn to his article *The Stumbling of the Church and the Time of the Coming of the Lord*. In this article, he asserts that what delays the Lord's *parousia* is the internal frailty of the Church and its deficiency in divine revelation, stating:

What delays the coming of Christ is the absence of revelation and the weakness of revelatory knowledge that opens us up to Christ personally. The Apostle Paul affirmed this when describing the true and proper end goal of the Church: "till we all come to the unity of the faith and of the knowledge of the Son of God, to a perfect man, to the measure of the stature of the fullness of Christ" (Eph. 4:13). When the Church reaches the fullness of Christ, becoming like Him, she will have fulfilled her mission in the world. John emphasizes this by saying: "But we know that when He is revealed, we shall be like Him, for we shall see Him as He is" (1 John 3:2).[15]

---

[14] *Infra*, 80.

[15] *Taṯṯurāt al-kanīsa wa-mī'ād maǧī' al-rabb* ("The Stumbling

This theme carries through in the present book, where Fr. Matthew proclaims that the Church is entrusted with revealing the essence of "true humanity" to the world. He writes:

> If we fathom the depth of the Church, we conclude that when the Church is perfected and manifested in her glory and splendor, we will see in her the true humanity, the humanity as God intended to create it... This is the Church! She is the body of Christ, in which Christ will be the head of that one human being.[16]

From his contemplation of transcendence over time to his profound reflections on the *parousia*, Fr. Matthew reveals himself as a profoundly eschatological writer. His vision is never confined to the temporal but is always directed toward the ultimate fulfillment—the *éschaton*—where humanity will be united with their Beloved in the fullness of divine glory.

The Church, the Mystical Body of Christ

Fr. Matthew frequently employs the phrase "The Church, the Mystical Body of Christ" throughout this book. But what does he mean by this expression? When he describes the Church as "mystical body," he does not suggest something abstract or detached from reality. Rather, he presents the Church as a real, living, tangible, and universal body, deeply rooted in both the seen and unseen dimensions

---

of the Church and the Time of the Coming of the Lord"), Murqus Review, October 2002, St. Macarius Monastery, Wadi El Natrun, Egypt, 7.

[16] *Infra*, 128.

of existence. For Fr. Matthew, the term "mystical" signifies the Church's participation in the divine nature—a reality that transcends human perception yet becomes manifest through the mysteries of the Church and is profoundly experienced in the lives of believers. He underscores that the Church is not merely an earthly institution but a theanthropic being—both human and divine. Through Baptism and Eucharist, believers are united with Christ, becoming members of this mystical body, which, though invisible to the physical eye, is made perceptible through the mysteries of the Church. To put it in his own words: "The Church is a living, universal being. She is the mystical body of Christ, and her members are the believers who worship in Spirit and Truth (cf. John 4:24)."[17] He also states elsewhere:

> That is why we say that the Church is the body of Christ, and He Himself is her head. This is not just a simile or a metaphor but a living reality, because Christ truly lives in every member, as it is written 'it is no longer I who lives, but Christ who lives in me' (Gal. 2:20).[18]

Thus, the mysteries of Baptism and Eucharist are not merely acts of faith but sacred gateways through which the faithful are drawn into the very life of Christ. Through these mysteries, believers become members of this "mystical body" that transcends time and space, uniting them with Christ and with one another in a communion that is both mystical but yet profoundly real. He underscores this fact, stating:

> When believers are baptized and eat the body and blood of the

---

[17] *Infra*, 41.
[18] *Infra*, 102.

Lord, they unite with the mystical body of Christ. As the Lord says, 'He who feeds on Me will live because of Me' (John 6:57). They become living, firm, harmonious members, united together in His body.[19]

For Fr. Matthew, the Church is not a fragmented entity divided between heaven and earth; rather, she is a single, undivided reality that gathers all creation into communion with God. As "the mystical body of Christ," the Church is a living, cosmic organism, ever moving toward its Creator, drawing all things into the fullness of divine life. Building on this understanding, Fr. Matthew poses a crucial question:

> What then is the connection between the mystical body of Christ in the Church and His body that is in heaven, sitting at the right hand of God? It is one undivided body in heaven and on earth.[20]

Fr. Matthew explicitly asserts that union with the body of Christ is the central purpose of the New Testament when he states:

> We now behold the greatest spiritual principle that has been revealed to the saints of God from the time of Adam until today. We can consider it as the core of the doctrine of salvation in the New Testament.[21]

Everything Christ did in the flesh was for our sake and our salvation, as we proclaim in the Creed: "for us and for our salvation." In Him, we were carried, redeemed, and re-

---

[19] *Infra*, 87.
[20] *Infra*, 90.
[21] *Infra*, 87.

stored, for His incarnate life was not lived in isolation but as a mystery of union, drawing all humanity into Himself. He clarifies this idea, affirming:

> If you believe that God appeared in the body, and that this body died on the cross, and that this death was for you, then this death becomes yours. You can also say that you are affected by His death, or in other words, that His death is filled up in you (cf. Col. 1:24) because it was finished for your sake (cf. John 29:30).[22]

His Ecumenical Lens

The final theme we wish to highlight is Fr. Matthew's deep and unwavering commitment to the unity of believers, a subject he addresses extensively in this book as well as throughout his other writings. He was a steadfast advocate for communion within the Church, emphasizing two fundamental points. First, he firmly upheld the reality of a tangible and organic unity among the members of the one body of Christ, a unity that is not merely conceptual but is rooted in their living union with Christ, the head of the Church. Second, he underscored the indispensable role of the Holy Spirit in this sacred work, viewing the Holy Spirit as the very soul of the Church's unity. For Fr. Matthew, this unity is neither abstract nor symbolic but a vital and living reality, made manifest in the Church's very existence and expressed through her mysteries and spiritual communion. He emphasizes this living unity, explaining:

> When we encounter the Church in the present, we do not

---

[22] *Infra*, 88.

stand in front of a symbolic or blind philosophical unity, but rather we encounter a living unity because the Spirit of the Church flows in her members.[23]

Here, Fr. Matthew dismisses the idea of unity as a mere concept and stresses that it is a dynamic experience brought to life by the Holy Spirit. However, this unity does not mean uniformity. Fr. Matthew insists that the Church not only acknowledges but celebrates diversity, each member retaining their distinct identity, tradition, and role within the Body of Christ. He underscores this distinction succinctly, declaring:

> To fully comprehend the essence of true unity, we must discard the notion of leveling member disparities. We should avoid attempts to eliminate diversity, distinctiveness, and specialized functions that are necessary to make a cohesive entity.[24]

As he clarifies in another book, the role of the Holy Spirit in fostering unity is not to erase individuality but to sanctify and harmonize it for the greater good. The Spirit unites diverse personalities in love, weaving their unique gifts into the fabric of the Church, so that each member, in their distinctiveness, contributes to her enrichment and growth:

> The Holy Spirit is the one who unites thoughts; there is no way for people to meet in the true Christ unless they first meet in the Spirit on the level of love.[25]

---

[23] *Infra*, 113.

[24] *Infra*, 114.

[25] Matthew the Poor, "The Paraclete," in Id., *al-Rūḥ al-qudus*

He further elaborates on this dynamic work of the Spirit, stating:

> We find that the Holy Spirit works to create distinct personalities by granting one person something He does not give to another. He distributes tasks according to individual gifts, but with wisdom and measure, so that from these distinctions, a unity is achieved—a unity of work and edification—all aimed at one purpose, the fulfillment of this one mystical body, that is, the Church.[26]

Invitation to Join this Unique Journey

As you embark on this reading journey, we invite you to approach it with a prayerful and contemplative heart, as though stepping beyond time to enter the tent of the covenant in the wilderness of Sinai, the temple in Jerusalem, or even gathering with the early believers in the catacombs of Rome. May this book be a source of blessing and illumination, deepening our understanding of the Church as the Mystical Body of Christ and drawing us ever closer to the divine mystery of His presence. As you reach the final pages of this book, we hope you will come to see the Church as Fr. Matthew the Poor saw her—a mystical, divine, living reality that transcends time and space, yet remains deeply embedded in our lived experience.

Fr. Matthew does not merely call us to understand the Church with our minds; he invites us to enter into her life

---

al-rabb al-muḥyī ("The Holy Spirit, the Life-Giving Lord"), vol. 2 (Egypt: Saint Macarius Monastery, 2020), 534.

[26] Matthew the Poor, "The Pentecost," in Id., *al-Rūḥ al-qudus al-rabb al-muḥyī*, 195.

with our whole being, to become living members of the body of Christ, united in the Spirit and alive in faith. The journey of reading this book, much like the journey of the Church herself, passes through suffering and tribulation, through the wilderness of Sinai. Yet, it ultimately leads to the most profound encounter of all, beholding the Lord face to face and entering into perfect and eternal union with our Beloved, our Lord Jesus Christ.

EDITORIAL NOTE

St. Macarius Press is pleased to introduce a new series about the Church, called *Ecclesia*. The first volume in this series is the book you are holding, *His Body: The Church Immortal,* by our late beloved Father Matthew the Poor. The second volume, *The Mystery of Unity: Writings on Ecumenism,* will follow, and a third volume, containing more articles and homilies on the same topic, is currently in the making.

Before you delve into this unique book, we would like to highlight a few important notes. Originally written in 1959, this book was translated almost 35 years ago and had undergone many edits to make it readable for modern readers, accessible to a Western audience, and faithful to the original Arabic text. Due to the fact that Fr. Matthew the Poor extensively utilized Arabic literary techniques, which often involve the repetition and recurrence of ideas, we have endeavored to minimize these aspects in this translation.

We did not adhere to the original chapter order during the translation process. We tried to collect and organize ideas and thoughts under one title. We take almost all biblical verses from the New King James Version (NKJV); if we use another version, we will indicate it. Fr. Matthew relies deeply on the Arabic version of the Bible by Smith and Van Dyck (ARB) and, in a few instances, uses the Septuagint in the Old Testament quotes. All the notes are provided by the translators.

Acknowledgments

The Monastery of St. Macarius is deeply grateful to all those who contributed to bringing this treasure to light. We extend our heartfelt thanks to Metropolitan Saba (Isper), Archbishop of New York and Metropolitan of the Antiochian Orthodox Christian Archdiocese of North America, for graciously accepting our request to write the foreword despite his busy schedule and numerous pastoral responsibilities. May the Lord reward him abundantly.

Special thanks to Monk Pijimi al-Maqari, who laid the initial groundwork for this translation and patiently waited for many years until the book came to fruition. We also remember the late Fuad Andrawis and his daughter, Nabila Andrawis, who spent a whole week in the guesthouse diligently working on the first translated draft of this project.

We thank John Ehab and Joanna Silosky from The Antiochian Orthodox Church in Colorado, who revised and edited the book, and Michel from the USA, who also contributed to the editing process. We are grateful to George Makary from Canada, who created a beautiful icon depicting and explaining the entire book for the front cover; to David Georgy from Australia for designing the book cover; and to all those who helped us but prefer to remain unnamed. May the Lord reward them all.

Lastly, we extend our heartfelt gratitude to all who continuously support and encourage us in this sacred mission of spreading the words and teachings of Fr. Matthew the Poor. Your unwavering encouragement is deeply appreciated.

HIS BODY
THE CHURCH IMMORTAL

PREFACE

BY FATHER MATTHEW THE POOR

In the introduction to the book "The Orthodox Prayer Life," we discussed the scarcity and dryness in spiritual life that the Coptic Church is currently suffering of. The Church needs a generation that truly tastes asceticism, worship, and mysticism that represent the essence of Orthodoxy. We believe that the book has shed some light on the ancient paths once walked by the saints, clearing away the neglect, ignorance, and forgetfulness that had accumulated over thirteen centuries. We are almost certain that footsteps have begun to tread those same paths once again.

Necessity has compelled me to write the current book, "The Immortal Church," since those walking on the paths of salvation cannot do without knowing their own Church as a source of light essential for the way. However, the primary reason for writing this book, undoubtedly, is the overwhelming sense of what believers in this age are suffering from: an intellectual laziness that has afflicted the Church. The minds of her leaders have grown indifferent to in-depth studies of the Holy Scriptures, resulting in the cessation of the Holy Spirit's flow of intellectual production, whether in preaching or writing. Theological concepts have shrunk within a narrow framework of memorized knowledge without finding an outlet in behavior. Preachers, and even academics, avoid talking about theology, and if they do, it is with caution and trembling. They adhere to memorized words whose meanings have dried up in the minds of the listeners due to their lack of harmony with the actual feelings in human life. Thus, the Church has become theologically impoverished; teachings have become contradictory and uncontrolled, and evangelism has been confined to narrow circles that do not intersect but rather aim at goals that are not of the Spirit of the Church and are far removed from salvation; therefore, we do not see the Church bearing fruit because she does not work for the sake of Christ.

We call for an intellectual revival and theological awareness based on rediscovering our rights in the person of Christ, so we may receive from Him "grace and truth" (John 1:17), and come to know our free salvation in the communion of His divinity. Thus, the Church will regain her divine life according to her original Orthodox path, and believers will be united again in thought, faith, and prayer.

Let the reader know that the diseases of this generation, whether social, psychological, economic, or even physical, all arise from a disturbance in the relationships that bind humankind to God. These can only be treated through the treatment of the human spirit which can only be treated with abundant theological doses.

This book is at a living theological level, easy in its meaning and style, because theology, in my view, is easier and closer to the human soul than any other science, as long as it stems from the reality of feeling, experience, and behavior, not from the reality of logic, measurement, or dialectical proof.

What is the Church? Is the Church merely a gathering of believers in a place at a certain time, as some scholastics might say? No. The Church is a living, universal being. She is the mystical body of Christ, and her members are the believers who worship in Spirit and Truth (cf. John 4:24). She is constantly growing towards a goal set for her before the ages, and she moves without stopping or regressing. Her past is alive, and her future is always present. Within her, time is transformed into wisdom, pain into testimony, and distress into faith. Suffering is not alien to the Church's nature, nor does she consider it to be merely coincidental, because suffering was not put on Christ secondarily, but rather suffering was the ultimate goal of the Incarnation!

The believers united in her body remain alive in her, and death does not separate them from her, because her body is Christ. In fact, her members who lived in previous ages are still living in her and working with us, in the unity of the mysteries (sacraments),[1] and in the unity of prayer and mutual intercession. Those in her now are not considered to be in her or part of her unless they possess the Spirit of the Church inside themselves. The Spirit of the Church is communion with Christ and the poor.

Communion with Christ means a living faith that is ready to testify to the extent of shedding blood, and communion with the poor is a shared morsel. What else does the Church represent? Is the Church simply feasts, liturgies, commemorations, candles, incense, and praises, as some liturgists perceive her to be? Definitely not. The Church represents a living communion in the divine mysteries. They are

---

[1] In translating the Arabic term *sirr*,' 'mystery' was chosen instead of the more common Western word 'sacrament' due to its direct correspondence with the Greek word *mysterion*. The term mystery emphasizes the revelation of God's saving truth, love, care, protection, and presence (translators' note).

not formalities or religious ordinances that bear fruit by mechanically reiterating them. Instead, they help introduce us to the living God, pour out our souls before the altar, and completely prostrate ourselves at the feet of God in great humility and contrition. The priest presents himself as a sacrifice through prayer and, by his life and example, paves the way for the whole congregation to offer the sacrifices of their souls to God, free from the blemishes of selfishness and love of money and the world.

Reading in the Church is an entreaty, praise is an act of supplication, incense is prayer without blemish, candles represent intercession and faith, and the liturgy is an approach to the throne of God, a gate that opens to the divine fire, and communion with the Holy.

Feasts are a commemoration of tears shed and blood spilled, a call to self-sacrifice, a model of how to love, and a communion in shared struggle. With the liturgy, the Church paves a mystical, spiritual path for believers. By preaching and serving the Word, the Church enlightens their minds, so they are renewed every day through knowledge, being transformed by renewing their minds to reach through knowledge to eternal life (cf. 2 Cor. 4:16, Eph. 4:23)—which is the goal of all ritual and worship. As John puts it, "This is eternal life: that they may know You, the only true God, and Jesus Christ, whom You have sent" (John 17:3).

What is Orthodoxy? Does Orthodoxy mean theological theories and intricate dogmas that the common people cannot engage in, as some dogmatists assess? Not at all. Orthodoxy means a sound spiritual life. It is communion with the Father and the Son in a living faith. The Church's Orthodoxy is not about theological theories, but the practical application of sound theological principles. The

Orthodox Church is common people themselves understanding theology, confessing the doctrine and living the faith. Orthodoxy is just a word that means "uprightness" or the correct understanding of something. It is a word that can be used to define theories in physics and chemistry, and anything that could be deemed true. As for the Orthodox Church, she is represented by believers living an upright church life. She is the Lord's body, as we have known it and according to the truth. There can be no Orthodox Church unless there are believers who are fully aware of the divine truth, believe in the Incarnation with a sound faith and effectively participate in the Body, and then live in truth, faith, and the efficacy of communion in the Lord's body. Dogma and faith do not establish a Church. Nor will those who hold an "orthodox theology" or have an "orthodox faith" edify the Church. The Church is represented by believers who live an orthodox theology. Orthodoxy on an ecclesial level is a sound doctrine which is alive in the faithful.

What are the boundaries of the Orthodox Church? Does the Orthodox Church stand on a particular social group or a chosen people apart from the rest of the peoples of the world, as the fundamentalists see her? Nay. The Orthodox Church is God's Spirit in humanity's temple. She is, thus, all-embracing and universal, capable and ready to accept scattered people who have been tormented by negative trends throughout the world. She is an authentic, free and precious yeast, which the winds of grace carry easily through the faithful, who scatter it everywhere on the face of the earth. She is the voice of one crying (cf. Isa. 40:3, Matt. 3:3) that echoes in every spiritually desolate wilderness of the world, proclaiming the Kingdom of truth, love, freedom, and peace. Just as Christ is for the whole world and is its light, and as the gospel is for the whole world and is its lamp, so too the Orthodox Church must be a light without reservation or cautiousness, for the truth that is within her is Christ. If one fears for truth to be lost, then this "truth" does not come from Christ. The light that is within the Church is the gospel. If one fears for light to be overcome by darkness, then this light is not the light of the gospel. The Orthodox Church is endowed with the spirit of prophecy and is preserved for the day she is called to testify. When she becomes aware of herself, she will preach to the whole world with love, sacrifice and brotherhood, in the clarity of truth and the proof of spirit and strength. The Orthodox Church is a true revelation of the Kingdom of God, although partial. She is an image of the Kingdom in a mirror that becomes clear to those who understand it without prejudice. Day by day, this image will become clearer through ministry.

Father Matthew the Poor
'Amiriyya Desert (Egypt)
June 1959

PART ONE

SHADOW OF THE HEAVENLY THINGS

Just as the properties of the tree with all its subtle structure are latent in the small seed from which it sprouts, so were the properties of the Church with all her subtle details of faith, salvation and missionary work latent in the rites and offerings of the Old Testament.

CHAPTER ONE

THE TENT IN THE
WILDERNESS

Of ram skins [...] and badger skins (Ex. 26:14).

The foundation that God laid in the Old Testament was dug very deeply, wisely, and in various ways in order to hold such a great salvation (cf. Heb. 2:3), to which every human, people, and nation under heaven is invited.

A Tent in the Wilderness, or Features of the Early Church

Who would have believed that this simple tent (cf. Ex. 25-31; 35-40), covered with ram skins, goats' and sheep's hair, erected on sticks and pegs, carried on backs and shoulders, contained inwardly and outwardly the mystery of the Church and the salvation of the whole world?

Let us approach her with respect and reverence, for this tent was not designed by a man, but was constructed according to the pattern which God showed to Moses on the mountain, after he had fasted forty days and forty nights, going entirely without food or drink (cf. Ex. 25:40; Heb. 8:5).

Therefore, the tent was nothing less than a small, material, embodied image of a great, immaterial, spiritual reality that was about to be revealed spiritually, when humanity would ascend from the image to the truth, from matter to spirit, from naive childhood to wise adulthood, and from mental limitations to unlimited spaciousness in God. Paul gazed upon the tent through the revelation he received and saw that she was the "shadow of the heavenly things, as Moses was divinely instructed when he was about to make the tabernacle" (Heb. 8:5). The heavenly things, in the perspective of the gospel, are matters related to spiritual being and one's relationship to God. That is, the tent was an analogy for the link that binds us to God. It was a shadow of the reality of this connection, which would one day be revealed, passing from shadow to light, so that every person would know his or her place in God and the place of God in him or her.

Externally, the tent had no beauty that one should desire (cf. Isa. 53:1), for on the outside it was ram skins and goats' hair (cf. Ex. 36:14). As for the inside, it was decorated in different ways: with byssus (that is, blue silk), pure white linen, gold, silver, fragrant woods, fine incense, divine bread (cf. Ex. 25), and a lampstand. Concerning these things, we adhere to the limits of Paul's interpretation.

But everything in the tent, and even its name, was an explicit reference to the reality it expressed. "The tent of meeting," meaning the meeting of God with His people, as God Himself described it,

> [Is] where I will meet you to speak with you. And there I will meet with the children of Israel, and the tabernacle shall be sanctified by My glory. So, I will consecrate the tabernacle of meeting and the altar. I will also consecrate both Aaron and his

sons to minister to Me as priests. I will dwell among the children of Israel and will be their God (Ex. 29:42-45).

This is the first meaning of the Church, for the Church is not only a meeting of believers with one another, but also a meeting of God with the faithful. Moreover, it is attendance in the divine presence to listen to God and acquire knowledge of life. If we analyze the rituals that the priests and people were required to practice in the tent, we will find that they all aimed towards one goal—God's presence among His people.

God's Presence in the Tent

Before the advent of the Church, it was not easy for God to dwell among a people, especially if we consider that they did not know Him (cf. John 1:10). And if we saw the world at that time, we would find that people, in general, had been corrupted by sin to the extent that it became part of their very being, and a law dominating their members which became instruments of sin, iniquity, and impurity. Sin stirred up their animal instincts, so their bodies domineered over their minds and behaviors, and their lust for corruption was kindled. The result is that their thoughts were darkened and their hearts turned away from accepting the revealed truth in creation. Their thinking declined and degenerated to the point in which they worshiped insects, reptiles and beasts. And this was not the case for Israel only but for everyone (cf. Rom. 1:18-32).

For God to raise humanity from this miserable condition and free them from the dominion of sin and the darkness of ignorance, He had to start with forming a homogeneous unity, a people that He would gather under special restrictions and isolate from the rest of the nations. He would then teach humanity little by little, until they reached human perfection, out of which messengers could emerge for the whole world.

This is precisely what the Lord, with long-suffering, has done. He drove Abraham out of his land and clan to Palestine, blessed his descendants, and moved Abraham's children to Egypt. They lived there as an independent entity, but they gained wisdom from the ancient Egyptian civilization. Hence, they attained knowledge in all life's trades: agriculture, weaving, dyeing, carving, building, plumbing, carpentry, painting, medicine, astronomy, philosophy, and theology. Then the Lord set them apart in the wilderness, far from all influences, and began to purify and discipline them. And He killed all the generation that came out of Egypt, about six hundred thousand, except two who were kept for testimony: Caleb, the son of Jephunneh, and Joshua, the son of Nun. But the rest of their descendants were brought into Canaan after He had taught them to be an independent people with their own faith, rituals, customs, traditions, and names. Thus, the Lord completed the preliminary steps for forming a special people whom He raised, as a father would raise a child dear to him. Is the formation, upbringing and education of a primitive people much different from raising a human soul or child? If we follow the gradual approach that the Lord used in educating the people of Israel, we will encounter an authentic pedagogical method in all its aspects——physical, mental, and spiritual, in close harmony with the needs of the human soul——and we will discover the foundation upon which the Church is built.

Thus, the formation of the people of Israel and their preparation to accept the true faith in God, to know the first principles of salvation and redemption, and to taste a sense of freedom, was a field experiment of faith, truth, and freedom. The chosen seeds of this people were cast into the wide soil of the world, where they grew and became food for humanity.

God did not favor Israel when He chose it, nor was He inequitable towards the rest of the peoples when He neglected them for a time. In fact, the whole world was chosen in Israel. All peoples were represented in it. Israel was a representative of mankind which was being prepared to become its leaven.

God prepared His people for His divine presence. We read in the books of Exodus, Leviticus, and Numbers many precise commandments, statutes, and rites that Moses, Aaron, Aaron's sons, the Levites, and the rest of the people were obligated to perform in the presence of God in the tent of meeting, which could be summarized in three operations: purification by water, consecration by the anointing oil, and sanctification by blood. These three elements have been important and necessary since the first day it was given to humankind to exist as a people or group in the presence of the Almighty God. By the same elements, the Church fulfills purification, consecration, and sanctification until today. It was also necessary that in the tent there should be a veil and a mediator. The veil obscured the Holy of Holies, where the Ark of the Covenant was kept. By its covering God spoke to the mediator, whether it was Moses or the High Priest, who must have first performed the purification, consecration, and sanctification. The mediator had to have blood on his hands in order to pass between the people and God behind the veil. Even now, as long as there is sin, there must be water, oil, blood, a veil, and a mediator.

The first encounter between God and the Church took place when the primitive tent was set up in the wilderness, with its rough skins and constantly shifting location upon sand. This encounter represented God's acquisition of the first Church for all humankind, the stiff-necked people of Israel's rough church of the wilderness. Israel represents every people, indeed every soul, at the moment God meets her for the first time as a lost wanderer in the wilderness of the world, defiled in her sins.

In the book of Ezekiel, God describes this particular encounter and tells by analogy and symbolism the story of the early Church, or the humiliated and despised soul, and the persecuted people fleeing from the yoke of slavery and its cruel dominion. In this passage, we read how God found this people, how He opened His heart to it, and how He betrothed it to Himself:

"As for your nativity, on the day you were born your navel cord was not cut, nor were you washed in water to cleanse you; you were not rubbed with salt nor wrapped in swaddling cloths. No eye pitied you, to do any of these things for you, to have compassion on you; but you were thrown out into the open field, when you yourself were loathed on the day you were born. And when I passed by you and saw you struggling in your own blood, I said to you in your blood, 'Live!' Yes, I said to you in your blood, 'Live!' I made you thrive like a plant in the field; and you grew, matured, and became very beautiful. Your breasts were formed, your hair grew, but you were naked and bare. When I passed by you again and looked upon you, indeed your time was the time of love; so I spread My wing over you and covered your nakedness. Yes, I swore an oath to you and entered into a covenant with you, and you became

Mine," says the Lord God. "Then I washed you in water; yes, I thoroughly washed off your blood, and I anointed you with oil. I clothed you in embroidered cloth and gave you sandals of badger skin; I clothed you with fine linen and covered you with silk. I adorned you with ornaments, put bracelets on your wrists, and a chain on your neck. And I put a jewel in your nose, earrings in your ears, and a beautiful crown on your head" (Ezek. 16:4-12).

This is the story of the first Church: the people of Israel, who were born without a country in the wilderness (expressed by "mother"), and without a house (expressed by "father"), but the Lord found them, and chose them as a people, dwelt in the midst of them, gave them a covenant, and joined Himself to them, so they were named after Him: God's chosen people. He washed away the impurities of their deeds, He cured them of their diseases and ailments, and clothed them with knowledge, expressed by "gold" (cf. Rev. 3:18); silk, which is the righteousness of the saints (cf. Rev. 19:8); and linen, the cloth of chastity and purity (cf. Rev. 15:6). He spread His wing over it to cover its nakedness, which reminds us of the leather clothing that He made for Adam, which symbolizes the Law. He clothed His people with a crown to express their entry into the King's people.

Thus, the description of the tent of meeting, with its rough skins on the outside and its adornment within, aligns with what the Lord has done with the people of Israel, as expressed in Ezekiel's allegorical account.

The Story of Every Church

Neither the tent of the meeting in the wilderness nor the story of Ezekiel was just a story for the people of Israel to read. Rather, this is a living and eternal reality, an expression of God's acceptance of the first Church for humanity. It is the story of every church that God encounters. Is it not the story of the church of Colossae, Ephesus, Corinth, Thessalonica, Rome, and Alexandria, and every church in the world? The day God encountered every one of them for the first time, when they were defiled by sin, the vices of pagan worship, and the abominations of the nations, He accepted and washed them with the baptism of repentance for purity, anointed them for re-birth, poured on them His blood for sanctification, and then made them chaste virgins without blemish or defilement.

And Paul, Apostle of the Gentiles, constantly reminded them with authority of God's work among them, because he is the one who betrothed them, one by one, to his Master. Hear him say to the Church of Colossae:

> And you, who once were alienated and enemies in your mind by wicked works, yet now He has reconciled in the body of His flesh through death, to present you holy, and blameless, and above reproach in His sight... having made peace through the blood of His cross (Col. 1:21-22.20).

And the Apostle reminds the Church of Ephesus:

> Therefore, remember that you, once Gentiles in the flesh——who are called Uncircumcision by what is called the Circumcision made in the flesh by hands—that at that time you were without Christ, being aliens from the commonwealth of Israel and strangers from the covenants of promise, having no hope and without God in the world. But now in Christ Jesus you who once were far off have been brought near by the blood of Christ (Eph. 2:11-13).

Thus, the tent of meeting—rough on the outside but beautiful, wisely decorated, with typologies and symbols within—wherein God dwelt with the people— was the prototype of each Church, the original image, which precisely articulated the connections binding man to God.

The Church's everlasting truth, which Moses witnessed on Mount Sinai, could not have been represented by Moses in a bigger or more original way. He drew the foundations that define the meaning of a church, God's dwelling, sin, reconciliation, and mediation through blood, i.e. redemption. He designed the spiritual seed that bore all characteristics, qualities, and features of the eternal and universal Church, which will emerge from the womb of time as a tree of life bearing thousands of like seeds.

The virgin, the daughter of Zion who was born in the wilderness of the world, without a merciful hand that pitied her, of whom Ezekiel speaks, is none other than you and me. We were born and lived for a long time far away from God, full of desires and lusts, enslaved to Satan and sin. The Apostle Paul describes this maiden in a shameful confession:

> And you He made alive, who were dead in trespasses and sins, in which you once walked according to the course of this world, according to the prince of the power of the air, the spirit who now works in the sons of disobedience, among whom also we all once conducted ourselves in the lusts of our flesh, fulfilling the desires of the flesh and of the mind, and were by nature children of wrath, just as the others (Eph. 2:1-3).

This is how God found us when He called and purified us by cleansing us with the washing of water by the Word (cf. Eph. 5:26). He healed our wounds by the oil of His mercy (cf. James 5:14), sanctified us by His blood, brought us in with His own, raised us up with Him, and made us sit with Him in the heavenly places (cf. Eph. 2:6).

Therefore, the tent not only included the Church assembled with the Lord, but it was also an expression of God's dwelling in the soul and of His making the soul a spiritual temple for His habitation, wherein the Holy of Holies is found. It is inside the heart that the Spirit of God dwells in us, speaks with us, and intercedes for us with groanings which cannot be uttered (cf. Rom. 8:26). It is also there that the Holy is found, in which is the living bread coming down from heaven (cf. John 6:48-50), the blood that cleanses our consciences from dead works for the service of the living God (cf. Heb. 9:14), and the lampstand that is the light, which reveals the Word unto the knowledge of truth (cf. Heb. 10:26).

Therefore, the Apostle Paul did not hesitate to reveal this mystery: we are true temples. He declares:

> Do you not know that you are the temple of God and that the Spirit of God dwells in you? If anyone defiles the temple of God, God will destroy him. For the temple of God is holy, which temple you are (1 Cor. 3:16-17).

Even if our body appears to be at odds with the meekness and stillness of the Spirit inside us, as well as the beauty of our soul that is endowed with the righteous acts of the saints, this does not hinder us, because the rough skins of badgers, goats, and sheep were also mismatched with the blue silk underneath them. In any case, the body is a vessel, a protection for the fragile soul: "Or do you not know that your body is the temple of the Holy Spirit who is in you, whom you have from God, and you are not your own?" (1 Cor. 6: 19).

The Prefiguration of Baptism Hidden in the Passing Over the Jordan

For forty years, the tent of witness kept moving with the people in the wilderness, until it reached the bank of the Jordan River. By divine command, the people stayed at the Dead Sea for three days, three days being the time needed to fulfill the Baptism of death. Then the order was issued to cross over, and they crossed to the bank of the land they were to inherit, Canaan, the land of comfort and of good things (cf. Jos. 1:11-3:2).

So, the tent crossed the Jordan River—the river of baptism, the river of death leading to resurrection. The people crossed over with, or rather through, the tent. For as soon as the feet of the priests bearing the Ark touched the bank, the Jordan River cut off in great glory, and the waters fled from under the priests' feet. The Jordan was torn apart as Christ tore death apart, the Ark came out, and the people went out with it to the other bank of life, as the Lord came out of the tomb on the third day. Therefore, a prefiguration of baptism was laid down accurately in the model of the tent in the wilderness. This model indicated the manner in which the Lord Himself would pass over death and come out victorious, allowing the Church and every soul to pass over with Him to the bank of Resurrection, so that He would inherit the nations— "Ask of Me, and I will give You the nations for Your inheritance" (Ps. 2:8)— and the nations would inherit Him also, "that the Gentiles are fellow-heirs, and fellow-members of the body" (Eph. 3:6 ASV).

CHAPTER TWO

ONE SACRIFICE: THE PREFIGURATION OF CHRIST'S SACRIFICE

The Blood

The blood in the tent of the wilderness was the royal seal by which everything was made holy and became holy to the Lord, without which nothing could become holy at all, even the High Priest himself:

> For when Moses had spoken every precept to all the people according to the law, he took the blood of calves and goats, with water, scarlet wool, and hyssop, and sprinkled both the book itself and all the people, saying, "This is the blood of the covenant which God has commanded you." Then likewise he sprinkled with blood both the tabernacle and all the vessels of the ministry. And according to the law almost all things are purified with blood, and without shedding of blood there is no remission (Heb. 9:19-22).

For the life of the flesh is in the blood, and I have given it to you upon the altar to make atonement for your souls; for it is the blood that makes atonement for the soul (Lev. 17:11).

Blood is life, as science confirms, and as God's revelation affirms: "Blood is the life" (Deut. 12:23; cf. Gen. 9:4), and "the life of the flesh is in the blood" (Lev. 17:11). So, shedding blood means giving life, and the one who offers his blood offers his life.

Sacrifice Without Blemish

The ancient rite emphasizes that the sacrifice should be without blemish; otherwise, both the offering and the one sacrificing would be rejected. Therefore, the priest meticulously inspected the offering in the daylight. He would inspect its members, one by one. Even after slaughtering it, he would run his knife through it on the altar, examining its entrails, flesh, and bones, to be fully assured that it was without blemish. Only then would he light the fire.

Indeed, this sacrifice refers to Christ, because He is the Lamb of God who is without blemish (cf. John 1:37; 1 Pet. 1:19). But we need to contemplate the expression "without blemish" and its meaning. The symbol usually points to a person and to his role as well. The ancient rite stresses that the sacrifice should be "without blemish," so that when the sinner stood before God, confessing his sins, with his hands placed on the head of his sacrifice, he would feel and be certain that God looked upon him through the 'unspotted sacrifice' he was offering on his behalf. At the same time, the sacrifice being 'unspotted' implied the sacrifice's capacity to bear the blemishes and sins of the person who confessed them, making the offering worthy of death instead of himself. Thus, the person would step out justified before God, freed from the sentence of death.

If we ponder the notion of the animal sacrificial system in the ancient Jewish rite, we find that it was adequate for its purpose, since its purpose was the mere purification of the body of those making the offering, exempting them from their death sentence. As for its reference to the sacrifice of Christ, it was very precise, for the sacrifice had to meet the following requirements:

1. The sacrifice had to be pure, i.e. it had to be made with animals proper for consumption, pointing to the eating of Christ in the Eucharist: "He who feeds on Me will live because of Me" (John 6:57). What was offered was not a human sacrifice, as the pagans would do, nor was the offering set aside after the sacrifice without being eaten, as the gentiles would do.

2. The sacrifice had to be without blemish; that is, the animal could neither be sick, malformed, broken, nor bruised, so that it would be acceptable before God. This is morally appropriate, for how can the sacrifice bear the sin of its presenter when it itself has a fault? Or how can the offering of the sacrifice justify its owner, if it itself is not innocent and without blemish? This condition also refers to the sacrifice of Christ, which was truly without blemish.

3. The sacrifice was an irrational animal sacrifice, i.e., a non-sinning creature. Therefore, it could be set as a substitute for the sinner who confessed his sin (cf. Lev. 5:5). The sacrifice's complete innocence from sin rendered its death as a ransom (cf. Gen. 22:13). Likewise, the sacrifice's inability to sin was a brilliant allusion to Christ, who never sinned and could never have sinned because of His divinity, which made Him completely infallible so that He could bear "our sins in His own body on the tree" (1 Pet. 2:24). One could even say

about Him that God "made Him who knew no sin to be sin for us" (2 Cor. 5:21).

Tedious Repetition

Unfortunately, sacrifices had to be offered daily, and their blood had to be shed daily. This was because the blood of goats and calves, being an earthly and temporary life, bore its natural corruption, preventing it from possessing a lasting effect.

The daily repetition of shedding blood was considered an admission of its unprofitableness (cf. Heb. 7:18) and a significant indication of the necessity for a living sacrifice to be offered once (cf. Heb. 10:10; Heb. 7:27), a sacrifice which death would not prevent from being perpetually offered (cf. Heb. 7:23), its blood remaining effective for ever and ever on account of its immortality.

Likewise, as mentioned above, the blood of these animals was only effective for bodily purification. This was because it was earthly blood, and its purity was not spiritual but only physical. It sanctified only the body (cf. Heb. 9:13), i.e., the human body of the one that presented the sacrifice on his own behalf. For this reason, because the body would return to its impurity, a new shedding of blood, a new and repeated sacrifice was required. As it is written:

> It was symbolic for the present time in which both gifts and sacrifices are offered which cannot make him who performed the service perfect in regard to the conscience (Heb. 9:9).

This tedious repetition indicates a clear inability and failure of this sacrificial system to accomplish the purity and sanctification of the conscience, the restoration of the integrity and purity of the soul. Its repetition was a sign and an allegory of the necessity of a perfect sacrifice to fulfill what these sacrifices failed to do. The Scripture says:

> How much more shall the blood of Christ, who through the eternal Spirit offered Himself without spot to God, cleanse your conscience from dead works to serve the living God? (Heb. 9:14).

True purity is not the purity of the body or what goes into the mouth, but the purity of the conscience, the heart, and everything that comes out of the mouth (cf. Matt. 15:11).

For the one whose conscience, heart, and mind are purified, everything becomes pure, and this will only be accomplished by a living, spiritual blood that penetrates the conscience and distinguishes the thoughts and intentions of the heart (cf. Heb. 4:12). A spirit of purity and holiness is sprinkled upon the person as the blood of Christ is united with one's soul, spirit, and mind by the eternal Spirit, through faith. Thus, Christ's blood sanctifies and purifies the soul, spirit, and body as well.

Let us redeem this divine right to cleanse our hearts and consciences with the blood of Christ, so that, when we stand before God, we feel that we are pure in Christ's blood. We are indeed sinners in ourselves, but we are necessarily pure in the blood of Christ. Sin is in us, but in Christ we are no longer guilty of sin (cf. Rom. 7:23; 8:1).

Multiple Types of Sacrifices

The first time someone read Leviticus, they will feel worn out and distracted by the sheer volume of sacrifices, the variety of names and categories of sacrifices, and the many methods of offering them. The ancient rite required this due to the reality of sin, hence it was inescapable. Sin is a multi-faceted problem, and getting rid of it is not simple. It needed the incarnation, suffering, crucifixion, and death of the Son of God.

The multiplicity of sacrifices, their types, and the differ-ent ways of presenting them in the Old Testament is not a narrative that can be neglected nor an old tale that has no place for us now. As mentioned above, the Apostle Peter said about sacrifices and those who offered them:

> To them it was revealed that, not to themselves, but to us they were ministering the things which now have been reported to you (1 Pet. 1:12).

So, the subject of sacrifices still deeply touches our lives, and all the rituals that the priests performed in the past are still relevant to our thought in the present. This subject needs attention, study, and contemplation. We should read again and again about all the kinds of sacrifices without any boredom, because in doing so, we will discover our amazing salvation and how Christ fulfilled all its requirements on the cross.

We will not present academic research on the rituals, nor a study about the Old Testament. Instead, we seek to under-line the solid foundation upon which Christ built His Church, and to present the many facets of the cross. In this way, we will lose none of our rights coming from the sacri-fice of Christ.

The Connection between Baptism and Communion in the Sacrifices of the Old Testament

Few are aware of the connection between baptism and the partaking of the sacrifice of Christ, as they are not two separate mysteries. Rather, they form one truth and one sacrifice in two acts.

Christ's bearing our sins on the cross and dying is the first action of the truth of the cross in relation to humankind and the principal action of Christ's sacrifice in relation to sin. For He "was delivered up because of our offenses" (Rom. 4:25), that is, He died to atone for our lives, which were dead by sin. Then, Christ rose from the dead, as He is God in Whom was no sin whatsoever, nor was there any deceit in His mouth, nor anything that might keep Him in death. Therefore, He rose from the dead by His own righteousness. This is the second action of the truth of the cross, and the complementary action of the sacrifice of Christ, because He was "raised because of our justification" (Rom. 4:25). He died because of us, but He rose because of His divine righteousness.

These are the two acts of the divine sacrifice "who was delivered up because of our offenses, and was raised because of our justification" (Rom. 4:25). We share in the first act of sacrifice through baptism, since baptism is an actual, faith-based participation in the death of Christ. We die with Him and are buried with Him when we are baptized in Him. We die to the life of sin and we bury our old body with sin.

Therefore, we were buried with Him through baptism into death, that just as Christ was raised from the dead by the glory of the Father, even so we also should walk in newness of life. For if we have been united together in the likeness of His death, certainly we also shall be in the likeness of His resurrection (Rom. 6:4-5).

As for the second act of the sacrifice, i.e., the resurrection from the dead, the resurrection without sin for the life of righteousness, we partake of it by Communion, when we feed on the living Body and the life-giving Blood: "He who feeds on Me will live because of Me" (John 6:57).

The sacrifice of Christ is one, but in two clear acts: the first is the death to sin, and the second is the resurrection for righteousness (cf. 1 Pt. 2:24). We cannot achieve the second act unless we have taken part in the first act. We must die to live; we must die to sin in order to live in righteousness; we must be baptized to partake of Holy Communion.

If we consider the various kinds of ancient sacrifices—such as the whole burnt offerings, the sin offerings, and the trespass offerings—we will realize that these two acts, namely the death to sin and the resurrection for righteousness, have very clear and definite origins.

For instance, the whole burnt offerings were offered after the priest had placed the confessor's sin on them, and they were burned entirely, without anyone eating from them, neither the priests nor the people (cf. Lev. 1:9). The whole burnt offerings represent the first action of the divine sacrifice, namely the death on the cross, which Christ accomplished after He bore our sins upon the tree. We partake of the power of this death—the death to sin—not by eating but through baptism. Baptism does not entail eating or drinking; it is a confession of sins, a profession of faith in the One who died and was buried, and an affirmation of this faith by the believer's own burial in water.

The sacrifices known as peace offerings were meant for

thanksgiving and joy, with no mention of sin or trespass (cf. Lev. 3). These are slain and consumed by the priest and people. The peace offering refers to the second act of Christ's sacrifice, by which we commune with His nature. We receive the power of righteousness that is in Christ's sacrifice through Communion, by eating and drinking, as we eat a living Body that has risen from the dead and drink a life-giving Blood that can raise us from the dead.

A Brilliant Stratagem Employed by the Liturgy to Affirm the Resurrection of Christ

The sin offering for death was surrounded by a ritual that was strongly linked to the life accompanying it, so that death would never be separated from life in the significance of the sacrifice. We find that on the great *Yom Kippur* (Day of Atonement), in which an atonement was offered for the sins of all the priests, the assembly of the people, and the sanctuary and tabernacle of meeting, two goats were offered for the sin offering: the first was slain and burned and the second was left alive, with the sins of Israel being confessed upon it (cf. Lev. 4):

> Aaron shall lay both his hands on the head of the live goat, confess over it all the iniquities of the children of Israel, and all their transgressions, concerning all their sins, putting them on the head of the goat, and shall send it away into the wilderness by the hand of a suitable man (Lev. 16:21).

In this ritual we see a profound prefiguration of Christ's work, as the ritual expresses the two acts of Christ's sacrifice, namely: death and resurrection. Although the symbol is singular, the ritual included two animal sacrifices because the goat that had to die would surely not resurrect. For this reason, it was necessary that another goat would remain alive even after bearing the sins of the people upon its head.

Thus, the sacrifices of the tabernacle draw the basic contours of Christ's work. He fulfilled it by His own sacrifice: "He has appeared to put away sin by the sacrifice of Himself" (Heb. 9:26). He granted righteousness for eternal life with His blood. The sacrifice of Christ has many meanings, with profound mysteries concealed in it.

The reader may think that we are stretching our interpretation of these rituals, going too far beyond their literal meaning. But on the contrary, although we find ourselves overexerted, we have only touched on a few of the things that the ancient Jewish rite keeps hidden for the active seekers, so that they may bring out of its treasures "things new and old" (Matt. 13:52).

How unfathomable is the mystery of the tent of meeting: its foundation, laid firmly and precisely to bear the spiritual building of the Church with all her mysteries, and the salvation that was fulfilled in her through redemption. The tent of meeting serves as the foundation of the tower of virtues— the virtues of the soul united with the Lord Jesus—a tower exalted beyond heaven.

CHAPTER THREE

FROM THE TENT
TO THE TEMPLE
IN JERUSALEM

The tent of the wilderness crossed the Jordan River, entering into the territory of the gentiles. St. Stephen described this transition in his farewell speech, briefly but in truly divine words:

> Our fathers had the tabernacle of witness in the wilderness, as He appointed, instructing Moses to make it according to the pattern that he had seen, which our fathers, having received it in turn, also brought with Joshua into the land possessed by the Gentiles, whom God drove out before the face of our fathers until the days of David, who found favor before God and asked to find a dwelling for the God of Jacob. But Solomon built Him a house (Acts 7:44-47).

Thus, the tent kept relocating in the wilderness, having no fixed dwelling place, as an indication of the pursuit of a better, stable homeland; that is until it fell into the hands of the gentiles. But even after it had crossed the Jordan into the land of the gentiles, the tent continued moving about until David, the man of war, wanting to build a house for God, established for the tent a permanent dwelling place. But because of ongoing wars, God did not permit him to build the temple (cf. 2 Sam. 7), as a sign that, as long as there was war, the Church would remain a homeless stranger. Solomon built the temple in Jerusalem, the city of peace, because he himself was a "son of peace." The kingdoms around him submitted to his sovereignty, and his enemies submitted to him as a prefiguration of Christ, the Prince of Peace, who came and defeated His enemies, i.e., sin, death, and the world. After Christ overpowered them and put them under His feet, He prepared for the Church a better, heavenly homeland, and many mansions in His Father's house (cf. John 14:2), the city of eternal peace, the heavenly Jerusalem.

Solomon was endowed with great spiritual inspiration and special wisdom to build the temple. All of its construction—all of the stones, columns, inscriptions, and architectural elements—had spiritual meanings.

The great temple of Jerusalem, which Solomon the son of David built, remained standing from generation to generation, waiting for someone to tear the veil of sin to reconcile man with God, break down the middle wall of separation between Jews and Gentiles, and abolish the enmity between man and his fellow man (cf. Eph. 2:14-15).

And in the fullness of time, the Messiah came. One day His disciples took Him and showed Him the buildings of the great temple with pride and reverence, but the Lord replied to them:

Do you not see all these things? Assuredly, I say to you, not one stone shall be left here upon another, that shall not be thrown down (Matt. 24:1-2).

How Did the Daughter of Zion Commit Adultery?

Let us return to the prophet Ezekiel and hear what the Lord did to the virgin of Zion when she was struggling in her own blood. He Himself took her and purified her:

> "You ate pastry of fine flour, honey, and oil. You were exceedingly beautiful, and succeeded to royalty. Your fame went out among the nations because of your beauty, for it was perfect through My splendor which I had bestowed on you," says the Lord God. "But you trusted in your own beauty, played the harlot because of your fame, and poured out your harlotry on everyone passing by who would have it [...] And in all your abominations and acts of harlotry you did not remember the days of your youth, when you were naked and bare, struggling in your blood"... "Woe, woe to you!" says the Lord God (Ezek. 16:13-15.22-23).

The prophets constantly referred to the people of Israel as "the virgin, the daughter of Zion" (Isa. 37:22), symbolizing the purity of the people's worship and their faithfulness to their God. It is known that whoever adheres to the Lord becomes one spirit with Him, as the Apostle Paul says (cf. 1 Cor. 6:17). Therefore, those who betray the Lord, worship other gods, and turn away from God in their hearts, desiring corruption and obeying Satan, are to be considered as enslaved to another, while they are still under the Lord's covenant. In the same way, a married woman having an affair is nevertheless attached to her husband by law. If physical adultery is condemned because it implies treason and a betrayal of the marital covenant, how much more spiritual adultery, which is the betrayal of God's covenant?

And yet the people of Israel were unfaithful, even after God embraced them, imprinted His name upon them, purified them, sanctified them, dwelt among them, fought for them, made them rule over the nations with His mighty arm, crowned them as a kingdom of beauty and splendor among the other kingdoms, and revealed to them His love. As the Lord says:

> "I entered into a covenant with you, and you became Mine" (Ezek. 16:8); "I remember you, the kindness of your youth, the love of your betrothal, when you went after Me in the wilderness, in a land not sown. Israel was holiness to the Lord, the first fruits of His increase" (Jer. 2:2-3).

After all that, unfortunately, the daughter of Zion left her bridegroom, her father, and the companion of her youth (cf. Jer. 3:4): "Can a virgin forget her ornaments, or a bride her attire? Yet My people have forgotten Me days without number" (Jer. 2:32). The people of Israel turned away from the Lord, enchanted by the abominations of the gentiles, whose rituals and worship were mixed with fornication. The Israelites erected altars and temples for pagan gods on the high places and worshiped them there:

> On every high hill and under every green tree, you lay down, playing the harlot (Jer. 2:20).

> The children gather wood, the fathers kindle the fire, and the women knead dough, to make cakes for the queen of heaven; and they pour out drink offerings to other gods, that they may provoke Me to anger (Jer. 7:18).

Yes, Israel betrayed the Lord: "Neither did they say, 'Where is the Lord, Who brought us up out of the land of

Egypt, Who led us through the wilderness'" (Jer. 2:6). Therefore, the Lord addressed them with great grief:

> "Surely, as a wife treacherously departs from her husband, so have you dealt treacherously with Me, O house of Israel," says the Lord (Jer. 3:20).

For the sake of keeping the entire picture in mind, let us pause here. These distorted acts of devotion, which the Lord called adultery—the worst form of fornication, namely the fornication of the spirit—are incurable. In fact, if the body is impure, it can be cleansed through repentance and tears but how will the betrayal of the Lord and the heart's turning away from Him be cleansed? Where does the spirit flee from the conscience if the body commits adultery? And if the spirit engages in fornication, there is no conscience to reprove it. The daughter of Israel is still addressed in the person of the Church, in you and me. The gods are many and their altars are erected in secret and in public. The god of money is worshiped faithfully by many churches and people. His altars are erected openly in bank accounts. The god of covetousness has erected lofty altars in the hearts of many, on which unclean sacrifices are offered to provoke the Lord. They burn mercy, meekness, and love in its fire. As the children of Israel used to make their children pass through the fire as victims of gods and demons, so now people forsake the Lord and indulge in their detestable worship. There is also the god of hatred, the god of revenge, the god of pride and arrogance, the god of fame, the god of dominion, and the god of envy. Many worship all these gods.

Therefore, let us examine ourselves and diligently search the mounts of our hearts, lest there be on them unclean altars, strange fire, or victims that cry out from our oppression, our tyranny, and our favoritism, lest we share in Israel's bitter destiny.

Pronunciation of the Verdict

God was very longsuffering towards Israel. We read:

Have you seen what backsliding Israel has done? She has gone up on every high mountain and under every green tree, and there played the harlot. And I said, after she had done all these things, 'Return to Me.' But she did not return (Jer. 3:6-7).

God was ultimately compelled to incorporate all of Israel's past and ongoing disobedience, to compile all the causes, and to pronounce the final judgment.

Then I saw that for all the causes for which backsliding Israel had committed adultery, I had put her away and given her a certificate of divorce (Jer. 3:8).

When was the Harlot Divorced?

How grievous it was to the God of Israel that Israel did not recognize the time of her visitation, that Jerusalem strayed from her bridegroom, insulted her husband, struck Him, and slapped Him on the face. She put the cross of curse and shame on His sweet shoulder, leading Him out of the camp to be killed. That is why He wept for her. He saw the day of her destruction, He grieved to death, and He mourned over her with a grieving heart.

When Titus (AD 39-81), the Roman military commander and enemy of the Jews, raided Jerusalem, entered the temple, and defiled it, the people of Israel thought that the Lord would be jealous for His house as in former times, so they cried to Him, but in vain. The Lord had left His temple and its veil was torn apart as an eternal sign. Holiness was removed from the holy things, and the Lord departed from His people. In the same way, the Spirit of the Lord departed from Saul and an unclean spirit overtook him (cf. 1 Sam. 16:14).

The bitter result was not delayed, for the great temple was torn down, and no stone was left on another that was not broken down, as the Lord had said. The Lord's words alluded to the dismemberment of Israel and their scattering throughout the world to live separated from one another. These words were a clear and explicit prophecy indicating the establishment of a new temple.

Between the Tent and the Temple

To sum up, we saw how the tent presents an image of God dwelling with humanity after humanity has been sanctified and purified by water and blood. Then the temple portrayed the impossibility of the perpetuation of human holiness as long as a veil or sin separates people and God.

We saw the tent wandering in the wilderness, and how this depicts the Church striving for a permanent homeland while she is in this world. Then we came face to face with the destroyed temple, and how it dissipated all hope for the existence of this homeland on earth.

We accompanied the tent as it was folded, spread, carried, laid down, and pitched, and how this state of instability was a prophecy of the pain and persecution that the Church would undergo in her struggle, or of the distress that the soul faces in the wilderness of this world.

Then, we saw the temple standing in Jerusalem like a

great mountain, and how it represents the Church in her last age, struggling with time, or the soul when it enters its rest and settles with God after a turbulent life.

When the tent crossed the Jordan River and became a temple, it gave us a picture of the transition from the old body to the new man through baptism.

The mist that descended on the tent during the daytime, and the divine light that rested on it by night, showed us God's meticulous care, and His eye open to the Church and every soul, day and night, throughout their times of struggle.

The temple's destruction heralds the departure of the Spirit of the Lord from the Church, or from the soul if she slacks in her fidelity to God or abandons her struggle for truth.

Finally, the loss of the tent and the Ark of covenant, and the destruction of the temple, prepare our minds for another temple not made with hands (cf. Heb. 9:11), another city, built by God (cf. Heb. 11:16), a movement away from copies of the heavenly things to the heavenly things themselves (cf. Heb. 9:23), from copies of the truth to the truth itself, and from a dwelling made of goatskins or of hewn stone to the "greater and more perfect tabernacle not made with hands, that is, not of this creation." (Heb. 9:11).

PART TWO

THE HEAVENLY THINGS THEMSELVES

Just as a tree sprouts from a seed, so that its qualities hidden as an embryo in the seed appear, likewise, the qualities of the Church appeared, and the subtle details of faith, salvation, and evangelization that were encompassed in the ancient rituals and sacrifices were manifested. However, in order for the tree to rise, the seed must die first—or so it appears that it dies. As for the seed that sprouted the tree, it has not to be considered as dead: the New Testament is latent and hidden in the Old, while the Old is present, revealed, and manifest in the New.

CHAPTER ONE

THE NEW TEMPLE,
HIS HOLY BODY

"Destroy this temple, and in three days I will raise it up" (John 2:19). These words were uttered by the Lord Jesus to the Jews. Unfortunately, they did not understand that Christ was talking about a new temple, a spiritual one, the temple of His divine body (cf. John 2:21). By the words "destroy this temple," He was referring to His crucifixion and death, thus ending the era of bodily worship in a man-made temple. By the words "I will raise it up," He was referring to the commencement—by His resurrection—of a new era of worship in spirit and truth. This was to take place not in Jerusalem, nor on the mountain, but in the temple of the living God who fills heaven and earth: "For in Him the whole fullness of deity dwells bodily" (Col. 2:9).

The Jews used to gather for worship in a tent made of skins, and later on, they gathered in a temple made of stone. The place brought them together, and the blood of the animals cleansed their bodies, preparing them to stand in the presence of God. The place was an important element in worship. It was only one tent or one temple, to which all the

Jews of the world would go to gather and present the sacrifice. Through their gathering in the temple, they were purified. When they participated in the animal sacrifice, they were sanctified in the body. When they left the assembly, they dispersed. Their unity was temporary, and their physical holiness was limited.

Can a limited place contain, within its walls, unlimited souls? We know, in fact, that space is determined by matter. How then can the spirit be confined to a limited place? The place can only hold bodies. As for the believing souls, they do not gather except in the great unlimited Spirit.

Can animal blood sanctify immortal spirits? The blood of an animal can sanctify the purifying of flesh (cf. Heb. 9:13). As for human souls, they are sanctified only by divine blood that penetrates their incomprehensible spiritual essence.

Infinite Temple

The tent in its inward and outward appearance, and the temple in its structure and character, were but a mere prefiguration of the body of Christ the Lord, in which the fullness of the divinity dwelled, united with Him. It has been given to us to eat of that body, in which we unite and gather.

Thus, the body of Christ became the new tent, and the invisible mystical temple, in which believers assemble and even unite. Since everyone in the Church ate of the holy divine body of Christ, His body spread in the body of humanity through every aspect of time and space.

The body of Christ is now alive on earth, as it is in heaven. It covers all ages with its unlimited abiding members, i.e. the faithful of every tongue, people and nation under heaven, both those who have fallen asleep and those who still strive in this life.

The tent has thus spread to the utmost parts of the earth (cf. Acts 1:8), and the temple has expanded to include heaven. It traversed the receding ages to encompass what was before time and the future ages to include eternity. This is the temple of His body risen from the dead, the Church, "which is His body" (Eph. 1:23).

God, who once dwelt among His people, came to be eaten by them. They now abide, unite, and gather together in Him just as the branches abide and are gathered in the vine (cf. John 15:5).

The Veil in the New Temple

The veil that separated the Most Holy from the tabernacle, and thus from the people, was woven of a multicolored fine linen. In this, the blue color indicated heaven. This veil concealed God's dwelling from humankind.

Conventionally, no one ever breached this veil, this gate of heaven, and descended, except the Son of Man. He also ascended beyond this veil (cf. Heb. 6:19,20) to the Most Holy, the heaven of heavens, the abode of God the Father, where He sat at His right hand to appear before the Father's face as a High Priest for our sake. As the letter to the Hebrew says:

> For Christ has not entered the holy places made with hands, which are copies of the true, but into heaven itself, now to appear in the presence of God for us (Heb. 9:24).

However, when the Lord was crucified and gave up His Spirit, the veil of the temple was torn apart, revealing the Most Holy to humankind. This instantly indicated the opening of heaven, and the Son of Man entered, appearing before God. And when the Son entered, He found for us eternal redemption, and lifted the veil that separated God from us. The veil symbolized the sin that Christ abolished by His self-sacrifice. So, we too have acquired "boldness to enter the Holiest by the blood of Jesus" (Heb. 10:19). We can boldly approach the throne of grace to find mercy by taking the body of Christ, the veil which concealed and carried the divinity torn apart on the cross, revealing the divinity by the resurrection from the dead. That which was once a veil became a new living path to the Most Holy, by which humanity has been granted the ability to see God in heaven without any barrier: "Look! I see the heavens opened and the Son of Man standing at the right hand of God!" (Acts 7:56).

Thus, Heaven and the Heaven of Heavens have become unveiled in the new temple. The highest Holies in the heavens have become joined with the humble Holies on earth within us. Is this not what we ask every day when we say in the Lord's prayer, "Your will be done on earth as it is in heaven"?

Abolishing the Barrier of Hostility in the New Temple

Heaven, as we have seen, is the veil and has become an open way, a new and living way for us through the body of Christ (cf. Heb. 10:20) that veils and carries the divinity. Moreover, the Heaven of Heavens is the true Holy of Holies where God the Father is, having at His right hand the Son, a High Priest for us, who always intercedes for us (cf. Heb. 8:1; 7:25). We have gained access to enter boldly the Heaven of Heavens (cf. Heb. 4:16) by the blood of the High Priest, the blood of the living divine sacrifice that was offered through the eternal Spirit (cf. Heb. 9:14). If all of the above is true, where is God's Temple to be found? The Apostle Paul offers us an answer:

> Do you not know that you are the temple of God and that the Spirit of God dwells in you? If anyone defiles the temple of God, God will destroy him. For the temple of God is holy, which temple you are (1 Cor. 3:16-17).

Thus, God's temple is no longer made of stones nor marble pillars, but rather from living stones, hearts of flesh, opened to the spirit, and luminous souls, and unshakable pillars of faith. In short, "You are God's building" (1 Cor. 3:9).

As for the middle wall of separation, the barrier of enmity which separated the court of the Jews from the court of the Gentiles, it was a symbol of the enmity between man and his fellow man. Christ pulled this barrier out, thereby reconciling the two in one body, His own body, with God through the cross, killing the enmity by His death for the two, i.e., Jews and Gentiles. He broke down the wall of separation between them, i.e., the law of Moses and the statutes of the Jews, so that His blood became a new covenant and salvation for both, making the two one, the Gentiles like the Jews in everything. As all believers partake of the same body and are sanctified by the same blood, all become one, as the temple of the one body, and everyone has access to God the Father with one spirit. All— everyone who believes—are considered one flock with the saints and the household of God.

Therefore, the prophecy of Isaiah was fulfilled, as the wolf sat with the lamb (cf. Isa. 11:6), and the lion fed with the lamb (cf. Isa. 65:25). Finally, dogs ate with the children (cf. Mark 7:27). Israel, in fact, was like a lamb, and the nations around it were like wolves and dogs.

Unfortunately, we witnessed Israel turn into a wolf, who rose against the Lamb of God and devoured Him on the cross. While He was groaning on the cross, Israel surrounded the meek Beloved, like a pack of dogs and rapacious beasts. David foresaw this happening with the eyes of prophecy and described it as though Christ was speaking:

> Many bulls have surrounded Me... they gape at Me with their mouths... for dogs have surrounded Me. The congregation of the wicked has enclosed Me. They pierced My hands and My feet (Ps. 22:12,13,16).

And when the Lord sent His disciples to the Jews, He commanded them, "Behold, I am sending you out like lambs among wolves" (Luke 10:3).

Through the meek Lamb who sprinkled His blood on all, the Lord let the wolves return to the fold of faith, one wolf after another and one lion after another. Saul, who breathed threats and murder like a ruthless lion, and destroyed the lamb fold beyond measure, returned, submitted, and entered the lamb fold as one of them. Paul even became a trusted shepherd over many sheep, because the Lamb's blood was sprinkled on him.

The Gentiles, who were considered dogs (cf. Matt. 15:26), "were washed, were sanctified, were justified in the name of the Lord Jesus and by the Spirit of our God" (cf. 1 Cor. 6:11). Thus, they entered and partook of the showbread—the bread of God—which had been forbidden except for the priests of the Old Testament. The Gentiles became sharers in the inheritance and body (cf. Eph. 3:6). Thanks to the One who killed enmity on the cross, "there is neither Jew nor Greek, there is neither slave nor free, for you are all one in Christ Jesus." (Gal. 3:28).

Thus, the new temple of salvation spread and infinitely towered up so that the ends of the earth could not contain it. The new temple will not either be restrained by time, with its immemorial past and unknowable future. A temple with one court, without partitions, like a great sheet let down from heaven to earth (cf. Acts 10:11), in which every people gathers: Parthians, Medes, Elamites, Mesopotamians, Judeans, Cappadocians, people from Pontus and Asia; Phrygians and Pamphylians, Egyptians and those from the parts of Libya adjoining Cyrene; visitors from Rome, Cretans and Arabs (cf. Acts 2:9-11); and the people of the rest of Africa, Europe, America, Asia, Australia and all the islands, and every name called under heaven. They are all living stones—"on which is the name of my Father," "my new name" (cf. Rev. 3:12), and "the name of the new Jerusalem" (cf. Rev. 3:12)— being built up as a spiritual house, a holy priesthood (cf. 1 Pet. 2:5),

> ...having been built on the foundation of the apostles and prophets, Jesus Christ Himself being the chief cornerstone, 21 in whom the whole building, being fitted together, grows into a holy temple in the Lord, 22 in whom you also are being built together for a dwelling place of God in the Spirit (Eph. 2:20-22).

CHAPTER TWO

MEMBERS IN THE TEMPLE
OF HIS BODY

Of His flesh and of His bones (Eph. 5:30).

We now behold the greatest spiritual principle that has been revealed to the saints of God from the time of Adam until today. We can consider it as the core of the doctrine of salvation in the New Testament.

This principle is summarized in the fact that when believers are baptized and eat the body and blood of the Lord, they unite with the mystical body of Christ. As the Lord says, "He who feeds on Me will live because of Me" (John 6:57). They become living, firm, harmonious members, united together in His body. This body with these members is the Church. But how does the believer unite with the body of Christ?

By Dying First with Him

When Christ died on the cross, He did not die for Himself, but rather for us (cf. 1 Cor. 15:3). Here begins the mystery of the connection between the divine body of Christ and the human soul.

If you believe that God appeared in the body, and that this body died on the cross, and that this death was for you, then this death becomes yours. You can also say that you are affected by His death, or in other words, that His death is filled up in you (cf. Col. 1:24) because it was finished for your sake (cf. John 29:30).

The body of Christ truly died. Therefore, you, by your faith, take part in the body of Christ in His death, and this is the first connection between the body of Christ and the believer.

This connection takes its strength and imprint by baptism through the Holy Spirit in a mysterious fashion. Thus, baptism becomes a seal of the righteousness of faith, as we are buried in water, believing that we are baptized for His death (cf. Rom. 6:3). Thus, we take in us the effectiveness of His death by faith.

By Resurrecting with Him

· But this same body that died is a divine body that cannot remain in death (cf. Acts 2:24). Even if Christ died because of our sins borne in His body on the cross (cf. 1 Pt. 2:24), He nonetheless rose from the dead because He was sinless.

Since the wages of sin is death (cf. Rom. 6:23), if a body is sinless and carries the sin of another, then it will die but cannot remain in death. Therefore, Christ must have risen after paying the wages for the sins of others. If I am united with the divine body in its death by faith and baptism, and if the divine body bore my sin in itself and died, therefore He will have paid the wages of my sin. Consequently, I must also rise with Him (cf. Eph. 2:6), for I have been justified regarding my sin by His death.

Therefore, when Christ rose in His body alive, I also rose with Him (cf. Eph. 2:6). My connection to His resurrection grew stronger, as I became alive with His life and eternal with His eternity.

We have seen that the strength of the union with His death is made perfect by baptism as a mystical seal of the righteousness of faith. The strength of the union with His resurrection is perfected by taking His living body, risen from the dead, and His life-giving blood, which arises from death. We became alive in this body, and we will live by His blood even after we die (cf. John 11:25).

Thus, the body of Christ encompasses the believers as its members, living by it in reciprocal abiding: they in Christ and He in them (cf. John 6:56). Hence, we have the word "Church" referring to the mystical body of Christ, the body visible in the believers. As the Apostle Paul says:

> And He put all things under His feet, and gave Him to be head over all things to the Church, which is His body, the fullness of Him who fills all in all (Eph. 1:22-23).

The Sign of Unity

Believers are not members of the body merely because of their faith or life but because of their spiritual gift. The members unite themselves with the body according to their spiritual role. They take their function in the mystical body according to the measure of the gift they receive from Christ (cf. Eph. 4:7) because of their union with the body or according to their abiding in it.

And He Himself gave some to be apostles, some prophets,

some evangelists, and some pastors and teachers, for the equipping of the saints for the work of ministry, for the edifying of the body of Christ (Eph. 4:11-12)

Therefore, the body of Christ in the Church, though invisible, is revealed and perceivable in the gifts that the faithful members receive.

What then is the connection between the mystical body of Christ in the Church and His body that is in heaven, sitting at the right hand of God? It is one undivided body in heaven and on earth. However, if His body in us is revealed and known in the gift, in heaven, it is revealed and known as the gift Giver.

Therefore, we understand Christ's person as having His head in heaven and His members in us. "For we are the members of His body, of His flesh and of His bones" (Eph. 5:30); "He is the head of the body: the Church" (Col. 1:18).

The Reciprocal Abiding

By mutual abiding we mean the interrelationship between the faithful members and Christ.

He who eats my flesh and drinks my blood abides in me, and I in him (John 6:56).

"[He] abides in Me." Truly, by eating of the body of Christ and drinking His blood, we become members of Him, "For we are members of His body, of His flesh and of His bones" (Eph. 5:30). By this, we acquire in ourselves His life and His attributes: "[he] will live because of Me" (John 6:57). So, His personal power that overcame pain, sin, the world, death, and Hades flows in us. Those capabilities surpass our human nature, and we can only conquer by those capabilities when we acquire them by the power of the mystery concealed in the partaking of the Lord's body and blood.

This is what it means when Christ says "he who feeds on Me will live because of Me" (John 6:57). This is the efficacy of the words "he abides in Me."

"And I in Him." These words contain a deep mystery. May God open our minds to comprehend its meaning. By giving us His body to live by, Christ has become united with us and we with Him. Because we received His life in us, our life is now felt by Him. This means our sufferings, hardships, tribulations, worries—all are not only known or visible to Him but also felt by Him as Isaiah foresaw it, saying:

> Surely He has borne our griefs and carried our sorrows... He was wounded for our transgressions, He was bruised for our iniquities: The chastisement for our peace was upon Him (Isa. 53:4-5).

As it is written by Paul:

> Inasmuch then as the children have partaken of flesh and blood, He Himself likewise shared in the same (Heb. 2:14).

He assures us that He knows our pain as a partner. He will no longer groan for us but rather with us and even within us (cf. Heb. 4:15).

For He did not forgive our sin only with a word, nor did He rid us of it easily and freely, but forgave it by shedding His own blood, by bearing it in His own body on the cross: "Who Himself bore our sins in His body on the tree" (1 Pet. 2:24). Neither did He remain detached from us, but He gave us His body, and we ate it. His body dwelt in us, and we live by His life; as we lived and dwelt in the body of Christ, we became one with Him: "But he who is joined to the Lord is one spirit with Him" (1 Cor. 6:17); "You are not your own" (1 Cor. 6:19). He is truly affected by our troubles, sufferings, and infirmities.

For just as the members are affected by the head, the source of their glory, honor, wisdom, knowledge, and distinction ; so is the head affected by the members. It bears their sufferings, senses their needs, and responds to them. The Lord's words to Saul, "Saul, Saul, why are you persecuting Me?" (Acts 9:4) eloquently bear this out. The groans of members on earth agonize the head in heaven. The affliction of believers torments the Lord. Such unity underlies the Lord's saying to those who are merciful to the poor, miserable, and destitute: "Inasmuch as you did it to one of the least of these My brethren, you did it to Me" (Matt. 25:40). The Lord's saying is not allegorical; otherwise, our unity with Christ, our abiding in Him, and our life by Him would signify nothing more than words. God forbid! Christ actually suffers the same sufferings the believers endure: "So He became their Savior. In all their affliction He was afflicted" (Isa. 63:8-9).

Another kind of suffering affects the Lord as a result of the corruption of some members:

> For it is impossible for those who were once enlightened, and have tasted the heavenly gift, and have become partakers of the Holy Spirit, and have tasted the good word of God and the powers of the age to come, if they fall away, to renew them again to repentance, since they crucify again for themselves the Son of God, and put Him to an open shame (Heb. 6:4-6).

Describing their fate, Peter says, "[they] turned from the holy commandment" (2 Pet. 2:21), while Paul describes them precisely as having "trampled the Son of God underfoot, counted the blood of the covenant by which he was sanctified a common thing, and insulted the Spirit of grace?" (Heb. 10:29).

The Scripture says that such people cause the Lord excruciating pain, as they renew to Him the sufferings of the day of the Cross, "since they crucify again for themselves the Son of God, and put Him to an open shame" (Heb. 6:6). For they lay the shame of sin upon the holy body in which they partook and which took abode in them. They make the body of Christ a partaker of their iniquity and uncleanness: "Shall I then take the members of Christ and make them members of a harlot?" (1 Cor. 6:15). Their bodies, after union with Christ, became members of His body: "Do you not know that your bodies are members of Christ?" (ibid.).

So, as they scorn the Lord's sovereignty and defile their bodies (cf. Jude 1:8), they disregard the blood by which they were sanctified (cf. Heb. 10:29). And not only that, as they openly turn from the faith (cf. 2 Pet. 2:21) and commit sin, contemptuously despising the Spirit of grace (cf. Heb. 10:29), they not only crucify to themselves the Son of God a second time, but as the Scripture says, "put Him to an open shame" (Heb. 6:6). They bring ignominy upon Him. They submit to Satan, honoring him more than Christ and the Holy Spirit. Thus, their work is as if they "give what is holy to the dogs" (cf. Matt. 7:6) or sell the Son of God for thirty pieces of silver. And when they deliberately commit sins, they put their shame on the holy Body, just as it was on the cross. Hence, it was said "they crucify again for themselves the Son of God" (Heb. 6:6).

The Scripture not only says "they crucify again the Son of God" but adds "for themselves" (Heb 6:4). This means they exclusively bear the responsibility for this act and its punishment. Just as Judas, who deliberately disgraced Christ and delivered His body to the cross, found no place for repentance. Repentance and renewal will be withheld from those who despise the body, blood, and spirit, "for it is impossible... to renew them again to repentance" (Heb. 6:4-6). As the Scripture says, "they eat and drink judgment to themselves" (cf. 1 Cor. 11:29).

Therefore, their punishment will be worse than their deeds, for the Lord, in pain, will cut them off from His body. The rotten branch is mercilessly cut from the vine, "Every branch in Me that does not bear fruit He takes away" (John 15:2) to be cast into the fire. The believers who turn from the holy commandment renew the sorrows of the Cross, the painful memory of Golgotha, and the echo of the voices, "Crucify Him, crucify Him," ringing again in His ears in Heaven. However, there is happiness and joy in the heart of the Lord for the abiding of the fruitful members in Him. As the Lord says, "By this My Father is glorified, that you bear much fruit; so, you will be My disciples" (John 15:8).

How exorbitant the price paid by Christ for such unity! How agonizing the burden of our sins imposed on Him! How costly our steadfastness in Him! If only we were pleasing members of His body!

I beseech you, reader, to pray for me and for yourself, that our fellowship with the Lord will be a cause of joy and comfort to His heart. O Apostles, O chosen pillars, O saints, O beautiful members, pray on our behalf, we, the believers, on whom the end of the ages has come, who are unpresentable members in His body, so God may give us more grace to be the cause of greater honor. Do not burden the Lord with new sufferings or scandals through sins or wicked deeds.

The Church Forms the Body of Christ

In the previous chapters, we dealt with the primitive patterns that pointed to the Church and the symbols which—as if in a mirror, dimly—establish the Church's realities. But when we reached the cross and the living sacrifice of the Son of God, we encountered the truth in its essence without analogies, symbols, or mediators. The Church moved from the copies of truth to truth itself; from a tent and temple to a living body; from stones, marble, and gold into truth, faith, and believing souls. We then found the Church to be living members, the faithful believers abiding in the person of Christ, the ones who form the temple of worship. Every member in this body performs a special work according to the measure of the gift he receives from the head of the Church, Christ. He obtains a new mystical life through the Holy Spirit that deepens his soul and strengthens him with power in the invisible divine body.

Let us then understand that in the Church there are no individuals, but members. Just as the hewn stone after construction is no longer a stone in the temple, but rather becomes a pillar, a wall, an altar, or a foundation (cf. Ex. 20:25), so, in the Church, the believers no longer live as individuals, but within a variety of ministries with a variety of gifts (cf. 1 Cor 15:5). As the Church's Spirit is poured out into all the members, it gives them a special anointing and defines their work. The Spirit connects the members with grace, completes each one with the other, and perfects all with the Head, that is, Christ. Just like the skeleton, when it gets covered with flesh, nerves, and skin, becomes a living body through the breath of the Spirit; so the members that were dead in sin and then filled with the Holy Spirit became covered with faith, truth, and knowledge. Yet, every believer has a special ability, knowledge, and faith whereby he differs from another, just as bones differ in length, shape, hardness, and the presence of cavities or protrusions.

The diversity of gifts is essential in building the Church structure, just as diversity is essential for the various shapes of the bones in the body. Believers complement one another just as the diverse bones are firmly interlocked in the skeleton, "knit together by joints and ligaments" (Col. 2:19). The Church holds together, with its parts supporting each other as in a human body: "So we, being many, are one body in Christ, and individually members of one another" (Rom. 12:5).

The hand of the Lord came upon me and brought me out in the Spirit of the Lord, and set me down in the midst of the valley; and it was full of bones. Then He caused me to pass by them all around, and behold, there were very many in the open valley; and indeed they were very dry. And He said to me, "Son of man, can these bones live?" So I answered, "O Lord God, You know." Again He said to me, "Prophesy to these bones, and say to them, 'O dry bones, hear the word of the Lord! Thus says the Lord God to these bones: "Surely I will cause breath to enter into you, and you shall live. I will put sinews on you and bring flesh upon you, cover you with skin and put breath in you; and you shall live. Then you shall know that I am the Lord." So I prophesied as I was commanded; and as I prophesied, there was a noise, and suddenly a rattling; and the bones came together, bone to bone. Indeed, as I looked, the sinews and the flesh came upon them, and the skin covered them over; but there was no breath in them. Also He said to me, "Prophesy to the breath, prophesy, son of man, and say to the breath, 'Thus says the Lord God: "Come from the four winds, O breath, and breathe on these slain, that they may live." So I prophesied as He commanded me, and breath came into them, and they lived, and stood upon their feet, an exceedingly great army (Ezek. 37:1-10).

The expression "very dry" gives great comfort to our hearts when we feel like dry bones and our bodily members are scattered everywhere. Ezekiel intended to say: "We have fallen into the sludge of sin. However, out of the dry bones, very dry bones, emerged the Church, and her living body was formed."

What a wonderful hope Ezekiel's refreshing prophecy opens before us! Indeed, our souls are overjoyed with it, and even our bones rejoice. For the Church's body is built this way: first dry bones—many and very dry ones—then a life-giving Spirit. However, the bones must draw near each other.

When, O God, shall the bones quiver and believers draw near to each other so the church may rise alive?

The Spirit cannot blow on the lifeless victims of sin, self-ishness, jealousy, hatred, and folly until they are covered with flesh, nerves, and skin. In anatomy, flesh refers to the muscles that allow organs to fulfill their function. However, in the Church, flesh refers to the member's personal power earned through genuine understanding, study, and ob-servance of God's Word. Medical science compares the nerve to a wire connecting the brain to the organs, whereas the Church equates it to companionship with the Beloved in one's inner chamber. Regarding the skin, it is the delicate, protective, and silky apparatus that covers all organs and adorns the body with charm and beauty. In the spiritual life, discernment adorns knowledge with beauty and equips the conscience with intelligent sensibility. Discernment shields believers from falling, calms them during hardships, and adorns them with glory and honor.

We thank God because He brought to life "an exceedingly great army" (Ezek. 37:10), namely the body of the Church that will fill all ages and every breadth, length, depth, and height (cf. Eph. 3:18); for she is filled with the Spirit of God, and the body of Christ fills all in all (cf. Eph. 1:23).

Once the members abide in the Body and live by it, they no longer represent only themselves but the whole Body of the Church; they affect it and are affected by it. Have you not seen one's body lying on the bed, sick because of a swollen finger? The body is no longer free from the finger as long as the finger abides in the hand, the hand is in the arm, and the arm is in the body; and the finger is no longer free from the body as long as it is nourished by the blood that comes from the heart and is moved by the tight nerves in the brain.

Therefore, the believer has become a church, and he or she has what the Church has as long as they are alive in her. Likewise, the Church also receives the life of the member in her body, so all that he or she owns becomes hers, not only in terms of strength, wisdom, spirit, and wealth but also in sickness, weakness, want, distress, and pain (cf. Heb. 13:3).

If one member suffers, all the members suffer with it (1 Cor. 12:26).

Bear one another's burdens and so fulfill the law of Christ (Gal. 6:2).

Thus, the members are joined together in the body of Christ, but with an invisible power that operates mystically, just as life acts in the vine through the sap that nourishes the roots, stem, branches, buds and leaves—all are united together, in spite of the diversity of functions, for the sake of the forthcoming fruit. However, the life of the Church is different from the life of plants or even humans. It is a divine and invisible life because it is the product of the Holy Spirit.

CHAPTER THREE

CHURCH AND TIME

Birth

Although the life of the Church is invisible, we see her work spiritually—and we realize it—when the Holy Spirit gives birth to new children from the womb of the Church through baptism. The Holy Spirit delivers them directly from the divine body, and they are considered a new spiritual creation

If anyone is in Christ, he is a new creation (2 Cor. 5:17).

Having been born again, not of corruptible seed but incorruptible, through the word of God which lives and abides forever (1 Pet. 1:23).

Not of blood... nor of the will of man, but of God (John 1:13).

Thus, the Church's children possess the inherent power to become children of God, according to their own wills. If they choose to abide firmly in the faith, suckling the pure spiritual milk, and their minds are constantly renewed in knowledge, they will become firmly established in the Head—i.e., Christ—after the image of their Creator:

[that we] may grow up in all things into Him who is the head—Christ—from Whom the whole body is joined and knit together (Eph. 4:15-16).

By connecting to the Head, believers derive their knowledge from the source of knowledge and truth, in Whom are hidden all the treasures of wisdom and knowledge (cf. Col. 2:3). And this is accomplished through the action of the Holy Spirit, Who takes what is Christ's and delivers it to them (cf. John 16:14).

Since the members are connected to Christ, the Head, they are all united together according to the measure of their strength and ministry, and Christ wisely leads them as the head leads its members. That is why we say that the Church is the body of Christ, and He Himself is her head. This is not just a simile or a metaphor but a living reality, because Christ truly lives in every member, as it is written "It is no longer I who lives, but Christ who lives in me" (Gal. 2:20). Similarly, each member performs a specific function to complete the work begun by Christ on the cross. Members participate not only in the work but also in the afflictions:

> I now rejoice in my sufferings for you, and fill up in my flesh what is lacking in the afflictions of Christ, for the sake of His body, which is the Church (Col. 1:24).

Continuation and Completion of Christ's Mission

Thus, the work of the members in the Church under the guidance of the Head, i.e. ,Christ ,is in fact the continuation, integration, and completion of Christ's mission, preaching, teaching, toil, and suffering; and indeed, the goal of His incarnation as well:

...for the equipping of the saints for the work of ministry, for the edifying of the body of Christ, till we all come to the unity of the faith and of the knowledge of the Son of God, to a perfect man, to the measure of the stature of the fullness of Christ... may grow up in all things into Him who is the head—Christ—from Whom the whole body is joined and knit together by what every joint supplies (Eph. 4:12-16).

This means that Christ's body still completes its work through us.

The Body of the Church Encompasses the Past and the Future

Since the Holy Spirit is the Life of the Church—the body of Christ—the Church extends into the past and future, just as it is in the present, because the work of the Holy Spirit is boundless. In fact, the Church includes members who have departed and are considered the victorious heavenly portion of the Church, or, as the Apostle Paul calls it, "a cloud of witnesses" (Heb.12:1) that casts its presence over us. All those members work for the Church's body and their work now consists primarily of praying constantly for the militant members of the Church.

Space and time cannot confine the Church. She exists on earth and in heaven, in the present and from the beginning of creation, because Christ's redemptive work reaches back through the ages by virtue of His eternal Spirit, and saves all those who have embraced His promises.

The Church encompasses an enormous number of members, as we can read in the book of Revelation: "A great multitude which no one could number, of all nations, tribes, peoples, and tongues" (Rev. 7:9). They are endowed with diverse gifts befitting a coordinated body controlled by the wisdom of its Head: "Some to be apostles, some prophets, some evangelists, and some pastors and teachers" (Eph. 4:11); "Grace was given according to the measure of Christ's gift" (Eph. 4:7).

The members' work will be relentless, whether those who departed and form the heavenly flank of the Church, or those on this earth still burdened by strife and distress. They all move toward one certain end "Till we all come to the unity of the faith and of the knowledge of the Son of God" (Eph .4:13).

There is absolutely no difference between members who saw Christ in the body and members who did not, or between members who preceded the coming of the righteous One, i.e., Christ, and members who will live at the end of the ages. Christ is revealed to all in different ways. "[Christ], who is over all, the eternally blessed God. Amen" (Rom. 9:5).

The Church is the same today as it was yesterday; and she is before Abraham in the person of Christ (cf. John 8:58) Who fills all and in all, the unfading light of the world, Who was in the world from the beginning, and by Whom the world was formed (cf. John 1:10).

Christ is the Truth that covers every heart and dwells in every conscience in a mysterious fashion. He revealed Himself to sages and was recognized by philosophers. He is the life that raised the dry bones. He is the Spirit that fallen man inhaled in order to rise and live forever.

How truly magnificent is the Church! With her members she is the full stature of Christ. With her teachers, she is a great mind; with her wise and inspired people, she has abundant wisdom; with those who are enlightened by the Spirit and by the Word, she has deep and extended knowledge; with her self-giving servants, she has a warm and burning ministry; with her devoted worshipers, she has kindness, prayer and love. She is this way because the Spirit pours a perfect life into her entirety which is perfected through the Head Who, by being connected to her, leads her to eternal life with the Father.

The Church is a marvelous representation of what humanity is capable of, when, by rising above itself, the Holy Spirit is poured out upon it and Christ leads it to Himself.

This is the harmonious, unified human society that arises according to God's purpose when the Church's members take the image of their Creator (cf. Col 3:10) or when they return to their original image.

However, until all human races are gathered in the Church's bosom (cf. Rom. 11:25), the Church will fall short of the ideal model. The perfect Church is an actual expression of Christ's eternal power (cf. Rom. 1:20) and divinity. Will the Son of Man fail to gather humans? Or is the good Shepherd unable to gather the dispersed members of the herd? Or does the cross—on which the Lord was nailed—fail to draw everyone to Him (cf. John 12:32)?

Church Transcends Time: A Living Past

The past is very much a living thing to the Church, for the members that initially joined her are still alive, present and active within her body. They constitute the cloud of witnesses surrounding her (cf. Heb. 12:1).

No other religious community or socio-political entity can claim to have a history as vibrant as the Church's. For them, the past is merely a chronicle of once-occurring events and individuals whose life and death are nothing more than pages in history books.

As for the Church, her past is ever-present and alive. Neither her events nor her characters ever die. For Christ, Who brought her into existence, is not only a historical figure but also God transcending time. He did not create her out of perishable or mutable elements, but rather out of His own divine body, which He gave us as bread for eternal life (cf. John 6:50-51) for those who believe and eat from it. As a result, they shall become members of His infinite body—the Church—to live forever. Even if they die, they will remain alive in the body of Christ in Whom they abide in heaven.

The Church consists not only of persons who live and will never die, but also of Christ's living words which are the foundation of faith and salvation. In them, there is Spirit and Life (cf. John 6:63). Heaven and earth will pass away because they are created from matter. As for His words, they will not pass away because they are the words of eternal life. They are unchangeable and unaffected by time because they are truth. They never become past because they are spirit.

Death cannot separate the members who have died from the body of the Church. What changes is only the kind of action they perform in her. Instead of ministering in the flesh, they now minister in the spirit. The appearance of Moses and Elijah on the mount with Christ, conversing with the Lord about His impending exodus to be completed in Jerusalem (cf. Luke 9:31), is a clear example illustrating that the members of the Church remain alive, ministering in her. Every one of the saints has a special gift to perfect a ministry, watching over the Lord's word to make sure it is kept alive and vivified by the Lord throughout the years in order to fulfill His promise. The Lord may even use them sometimes if necessary to appear openly on the stage of earthly life to achieve a special mission. This is why sometimes the spirits of the saints and the martyrs appear to offer great help to those who plead to them.

Thus, we see that the Church's past does not fade away along with her events, only to suddenly vanish into oblivion as though grasping at the wind. On the contrary, the Church's history is a timeless present that remains intact. This is why in the Coptic Church we chant: "As it was, and shall be, from generation to generation, and unto the ages of ages. Amen."

Those who lived in antiquity are still alive in the Church today, expanding the reach of their mission .It is as if we hear the Lord saying to them ,"Well done, good servant; because you were faithful in a very little, have authority over ten cities" (Luke 19:17). Their sphere of influence encompasses both the visible and the invisible, reaching even to heaven and, at times, to the earth.

Christ Himself—the Head of the Church—is the same yesterday, today, and forever (cf. Heb. 13:8). He leads both the earliest members and the newest ones in the same pattern, according to His eternal plan and counsel, achieving one eternal work with all the members (cf. Eph. 4:12-13).

Church Transcends Time: An Immortal Present

In the Church, time is composed of eternal events. The Church never sheds her past because she always fulfills today what she began yesterday. Every passing day grows more vibrant and eternal. But, rather, time strips itself morphing into immortal events, until one day, the Church will reach what Paul referred to as the "measure of the stature of the fullness of Christ" (Eph. 4:13).

The Church strives to attain the stature of the fullness of Christ. There is unity of faith and knowledge between the members of the Church. This means that, at the end and according to the diversity of their knowledge, and the degrees of their faith and their talents, they will reach what Christ achieved for the sake of man "till we all come to the unity of the faith and of the knowledge of the son of God" (Eph. 4:13).

Moreover, there exists a unity of action, service, and edification. The faithful's actions, abilities, and ministry merge with Christ's action and ministry "for the edifying of the body of Christ." Ultimately, they reach the stature of the perfect, mature human, not in their individuality, but rather in their totality, fulfilling with their various attributes the exact same purpose that God intended from the creation of man—to become "a perfect man" (Eph. 4:13).

There is a unity of holiness bringing members to reach the holiness expected of the "perfect man," which humanity has been unable to achieve individually thus far. This perfect holiness is the sum of all the good lives, behaviors, worship actions, and ministries offered to God, each one according to his or her own gift, "for the equipping of the saints for the work of ministry."

When all of this is accomplished, the Church will reach "the measure of the stature of the fullness of Christ" and fulfill her mission by perfecting God's purpose in her. At that point, the earthly mission of the Church will come to an end.

Thus, it becomes clear that the Church will continually achieve partial perfection every day through the actions of her members in science, knowledge, faith, ministry, holiness, and worship, until her form is perfected, which will be in

Christ: "[That we] may grow up in all things into Him who is the head—Christ" (Eph. 4:15).

Therefore, every day is transformed and sheds its temporality through the action of the Church's spiritual members. Each day enters into divine fullness and growth, working toward the perfection of eternity until time reaches its fullness. At that moment, the Church will have completely shed time to live in eternity, in the fullness of Christ.

How far from the truth and impossible, then, is what we sometimes hear from those who call for the return of the Church to her early days? The days of the early Church are present in her now! Our desire for the Church to return to one of her past forms demonstrates our unwillingness to accept today's wisdom and mission, and our inability to comprehend God's will in current events. The Church's present is an integral part of her past. To those who plead for the Church to go back, I say: the Church will not return to her early ages ,and even if she did, she would not benefit from it. For the Church carries her past alive in her body. Her past is the faith experience, testimony, knowledge, holiness, authority, and partial fulfillment of Christ's stature. Looking back means that we are not truly living in the Church's present, for her present encapsulates all her past.

The Church is progressing on her journey as a living, dynamic body, moving quickly toward a goal drawn before the ages and the fulfillment of a specific ministry in the fullness of times (cf. Col. 3:10). She does not accept any movement backward, and will not stop in her course. Whoever wants to walk with her must follow her at the same pace, by renewing him or herself in knowledge "since you have put off the old man with his deeds, and have put on the new man who is renewed in knowledge according to the image of Him who created him" (Col. 3:9-10).

If we want to walk with the Church, we must also put our shoulders to the wheel of her ministry by offering our money, effort and thought. We must carry along with an enlarged heart and love all those who are left behind on the road, knowing that every service we perform will lead us to abiding and then to immortality.

Church Transcends Time: A Stubborn Future

The Church heads toward a stubborn future, as time appears to be constantly working against her. Yet, throughout her stands over thousands of years, she has triumphed over time and gained a living experience to utilize against time. She became victorious over the world as a result of this ceaseless, unseen war against the world's wickedness, philosophy, denial, heresy, ideologies, and works.

The obstinate future has surrendered and become a docile past. Time transformed into wisdom and knowledge for the Church. Her struggle resulted in fullness, and the struggle of her members resulted in eternity.

Thus, she accumulated vast truth, experience, and knowledge, enabling her to transcend the evils of time gradually and without publicity. She swallows death with her living body to become even more full and alive. The Church is above time. Everyone who lives in the Church is victorious, whereas everyone who lives in this age dies far from her living dominion.

What a grave truth that imposes on us! We have a serious responsibility regarding time. For, either we walk according to the truth and allow time inside the Church to grant us victory and fullness, to transform us through abiding into eternity; or we behave according to the whims of this age, not redeeming time (cf. Eph. 5:16), but allowing time to consist of nothing more than eating, drinking, sleeping, earning, science, fame, and entertainment. We cause the Church to miss out on living chances due to our dead and lapsed membership. Our lives lead to dissolution and ultimately demise.

CHAPTER FOUR

THE UNITY OF THE
CHURCH'S BODY

Unity of Spirit

When we encounter the Church in the present, we do not stand in front of a symbolic or blind philosophical unity, but rather we encounter a living unity because the Spirit of the Church flows in her members. Just as the Lord breathed His Spirit into His disciples and they became a Church (cf. John 20:22), so the members are clothed with ecclesial power that fills them with faith, love, and zeal.

However, just as the Spirit of the Church flows within each member, so too does the life of the member flow in the body of the Church—her members—enriching her with his gifts.

Unity of Talents

The incorporation of believers in the Church is not entirely based on their numbers but rather on their faith potential, the coordination of their many talents, and the preservation of their numerous living testimonies, whether through blood, anguish, torture, hunger, nakedness, or deprivation. The Church will keep these testimonials in her heart as a source of unity for her children, from which each new member will absorb as much as possible. The faith of the disciples, the enlightenment of the apostles, the zeal of the martyrs, and the love of the saints continue to beat in the hearts of the believers who are joined with the Church's heart. This treasure kept for us in the heart of the Church runs through us and forms us in the image of our fathers, just as children inherit the image of their father.

Unity of Harmony

To fully comprehend the essence of true unity, we must discard the notion of leveling member disparities. We should avoid attempts to eliminate diversity, distinctiveness, and specialized functions that are necessary to make a cohesive entity. The perfection and beauty of oneness necessitate harmony among its varied parts, symphony among her distinguishing traits, and collaboration among its diverse specialties. This is achieved not via the imposition of limiting regulations but through a practical agreement proceeding from love and harmony.

If any human unity loses the inherent and harmonious freedom that exists between its components, it would dilute the particular features of each of its parts and hinder their growth. This unity will not become a living unity; but rather a shapeless alloy devoid of any identifying characteristics of its constituent parts.

It may seem to you that we are beholding self-evident facts. Yet, look how much effort and trouble this principle cost the Apostle Paul. See how many times his spirit was provoked within him, writing that the Church must have distinct members (cf. 1 Cor. 12:4-30). He did not only write to state this as a factual reality, but also to remove all sense of jealousy, partisanship, and pride from among the believers. These defects severely plague the Church nowadays, so much so that they threaten to break up her unity, defeating her in the face of jealousy, partisanship, and pride.

Should there be jealousy among the members of the same body, or mutual recognition of their diverse functions? All members must be alert to preserve the identity, function, and qualifications of each other. Therefore, the hand that shields the eye, preserving it to maintain its identity as an eye, is worthy of being called a hand. Likewise, the believer who protects or even labors to secure the steadfastness of his spiritual brother in the Church of God, the body of Christ, is truly worthy of being called a believer. The eye that refrains from causing harm to the hand or impeding its work and ministry is worthy of honor. So likewise, the believer should reject any injury done to a weak brother in the Church.

But how shameful it is for us to talk about harm, injury, jealousy and envy among the believing members of the body of Christ, who loved us all while we were still sinners and gave His body on the cross for our sake! Is it not shameful for us to still talk about the first principles of how the Church's body is organized when we should, by now, be talking about the multiple fruits on account of the body's Head? Shouldn't this be our role because of the long time spent in the Church (cf. Heb. 5:12), our ministry, and the narrow path that we chose?

However, on the contrary, if talking about our weaknesses makes us ashamed, how much more should we be ashamed of the wicked deeds we perpetrate against the body of the Church! It is as though she has no Head who sees and suffers. I am afraid Christ has been crucified in vain (cf. Gal. 2:21)! The Church has travailed with us but given birth to illegitimate children (cf. Heb. 12:8).

What can we say? Every member who does not cling to his joint with the head cuts himself off from the body. This member begins to be jealous, envious, and hurtful toward others, "Vainly puffed up by his fleshly mind, and not holding fast to the Head, from whom all the body, nourished and knit together by joints and ligaments, grows with the increase that is from God" (Col. 2:18-19). The basis of Church unity is true and perpetual fellowship between the believer and Christ. This fellowship grows day after day and thus enhances her unity. The gifts of every member of the body of Christ must be revered. Every member's right in the Church and freedom of faith must be respected. Moreover, every member's efficacy in the body of Christ should be enhanced.

How miserable is that church in which the eye begins to rise above the hands or feet, in which the elderly say to the young, "'you stand there,' or, 'Sit here at my footstool'" (Jam. 2:3), and the rich scorn the poor by telling them, "Stand over there." When, do you think, will the Church know that Christ calls the poor and needy His brothers (cf. Matt. 25:40) as He sees Himself in them? When will the Church leaders do the same ?How long ,O Lord, will you not speak in the hearts of leaders about the sins of favoritism and bias, where decisions are based on personal recommendations rather than on real competencies?

The members of the body of the Church have begun to lag under the pressure of fear, cowardice, favoritism, injustice, and bribery. The legs began to do the work of the hands, if not the eyes, because the legs murmured and were not satisfied with the gifts allotted to them. They thought of themselves more highly than they should have (cf. Rom. 12:3).

In some cases, members who are still repenting and ignorant have sat on the teaching chairs, putting the body of Christ in danger of becoming all feet. A church that does not know the competencies of her members breaks her unity and moves forward without a plan or purpose. The work she accomplishes today will be destroyed with her own hands tomorrow.

PART THREE

THE PERSONALITY OF THE CHURCH

The Church is not a mere group of believers, but rather a spiritual body that has its own identity, nature, talent, and even personal distinct authority.

CHAPTER ONE

THE CHURCH'S
CATHOLICITY

We are accustomed to thinking of the Church as a community of believers. It appears that our understanding of the Church, or at least a portion of the community's understanding, is narrowly confined to the congregation we see on Sundays and feast days—a mixture of familiar and unfamiliar faces, known and unknown names.

Regrettably, this imperfect comprehension of the Church has prevented us from being acquainted with her living personality and receiving her spirit within ourselves. It has led us to forfeit our place within her sphere of influence. Thus, we have grown unaware of her genuine personality and, consequently, are insensitive to her Spirit, thoughts, legacy, and teachings.

The Identity of the Church

The Church is not a mere group of believers, but a spiritual body with its own identity, nature, talent, and even personal distinct authority. The Church's personality differs from that of the single individuals or members within her. It is not the sum of the identity of all the individuals or members combined.

The Church does not simply include her members. Rather, she includes Christ with His living person, body and blood, who is considered her head. She also includes the Life-giving person of the Holy Spirit who is active in baptism, chrismation, and in all other mysteries and gifts. The Holy Spirit is considered the Church's Spirit.

New Features

When believers gather, new spiritual characteristics arise, for it is not just a human gathering, but rather a spiritual communion based on familiarity and harmony aiming at common purposes surpassing individual interests. In this common experience, individuals influence each other through new-found reciprocal sympathy that could not have occurred within their individual consciences. The effects to which believers are subjected while united differ in strength and direction from the influences that subject each believer individually. Additionally, the existence in the same body of the souls of the martyrs, apostles, prophets, and saints who passed away makes the unseen impact of the Church as a communion of believers even more extraordinary (cf. Heb. 12:1). All these factors together confer on the Church a special personality and endow her with a strong spiritual presence.

The Church as a Mother

The Church is also a mother. She relates to each person as a mother does to her child, and even more:

Can a woman forget her sucking child, that she should have no compassion on the son of her womb? Even these may forget, yet I will not forget you (Isa. 49:15).

This is the Church who gave birth to her members. The Church is unique among all human communities, whether religious or secular. Other gatherings are based around a person, a principle, or a creed. As for the Church, she is a mother with her children, members of one body.

Again, the Church has her unique personality. If we truly perceive and fathom it, she infuses us with her spirit, imprinting her features on us, bestowing her authority upon us, and conferring on us the word of her faith and testimony. We, in our turn, will come to love her and unite with her, as the bridegroom is also united with the bride: "For as a young man marries a virgin, so shall your sons marry you" (Isa. 26:5). As a result, we assimilate her personality and reflect it upon the society around us through our faith and behavior.

Christ is Visible and Revealed in the Church

Though it is difficult to see the entire person of Christ in any one person, nonetheless it is possible to see Him in His totality in the Church. You may see, in fact, that every member reflects a characteristic or a gift of Christ according to what was given to them. As for the members together, you will see in them the likeness of the Lord (cf. Num. 12:8; Rom. 8:29) in the relationships that link them together. You will see the power and miracles of Christ, as you see His tears and pain. You will also see the truth. And behind Christ, you will always see the Cross.

When you look at the history of the Church—glorious

and awesome at the same time—you will easily notice the figure of Christ imprinted on its pages. In every generation, you will see Judas betraying love and the common meal, and Annas and Caiaphas fabricating accusations and invoking false witnesses .You will see the Scribes and the Pharisees always attempting to catch Christ in His words. Finally, you will see Pilate washing his hands and then ordering the crucifixion.

The Church was repeatedly killed. Yet, each time she was led to the slaughter—through her innocent children and teachers of truth—the person of Christ never left her, as He is alive in her and always persecuted, crucified in all who bear witness to her. Therefore, when we say that the Church has a personality distinct from the personalities of her members, we do, in fact, mean that she has a full personality deriving its qualities and features from the living person of Christ and the life-giving action of the Holy Spirit.

As for her body—meaning her organic entity—which is composed of all those who were born in her baptism, united in her body, stood fast in her faith, and saved, it is truly a spiritual body, with new characteristics not present in any individual member alone. These characteristics are not simply the sum of the characteristics of her individual members either, because the interaction of the members with each other and their union in feeling, sentiment, and faith creates new characteristics that originally did not exist in the members individually, as we mentioned before.

Unique Personality

The Church has a distinguished character, unique in its kind. Although her members are united in a way that Christ likened to the union of branches to a vine, the Church does not abolish the individual characteristics, gifts, and features of her members as she gathers them together.

The unity of the Church is reminiscent of and yet distinguished from the metal admixtures such as bronze, whose alloy consists of copper and tin. After the metals' fusion, this alloy bears new qualities not present in the original elements. At the same time, this alloy no longer bears any of the features of copper or tin alone, as it loses them completely in the forming of bronze.

As for the Church, while you will find new qualities resulting from the union of its members, yet you will still also find the qualities and features of each member, not overshadowed by the Church, and not lost at all by the union.

Likewise, the Church differs in the properties of her composition from the vegetal and animal bodies made up of living cells. We find that the vegetal or the animal body has new properties aside from those of the cells alone. Millions of cells merge together to give new unique qualities to the body while fading away for the sake of these higher qualities. On the contrary, in the Church we find that she retains the features of all her members along with the higher characteristics that she has acquired from the union of her members in her body.

The Church is not a Society

The Church is unlike any other religious or human society, either having political or social scopes. Other communities are formed around principles, goals, or persons; and these persons may be prophets, philosophers, or leaders that attract and inspire people. However, the principles, goals, and leaders remain separate from the common entity of individuals, as the belief is merely intellectual conviction, and only affects people in their behavior.

The Belief in the Church is not a Mere Intellectual Conviction

On the contrary, the Church is grounded in a living faith and her goal is a living salvation. As for the person who founded her with His blood, He is the living God. When attracted to the Church, we accept faith, not as a mere intellectual or sentimental conviction. Faith is alive within us because of the work of the Holy Spirit, who is a living, divine, and invisible person. Therefore, faith is united with us, and we with faith. The living salvation is obtained by the blood of the living Christ. When we unite with faith, we unite with Christ's blood. Everyone who believes will be saved.

Therefore, Christ has entered us with His own person. As Saint Paul says, "That Christ may dwell in your hearts through faith" (Eph. 3:17). As we unite with Christ through faith by the Holy Spirit for salvation, we become a living unit in Him. "But he who is joined to the Lord is one spirit with Him" (1 Cor. 6:17).

Yet, this union between Christ and us can only occur through our new birth from the womb of baptism in the Church. Thus, another union takes place with the body of the Church; namely with other believers.

The Catholicity of the Church

Thus, the Church is necessarily "catholic," meaning "gathering all in her," and not a mere society. Her members do not gather in her, but rather with her. The catholicity of the Church refers to her ability to give birth, or rather to her fertility, accretion, and expandability. The Church cannot expand to become catholic except by her renewable ability to give birth. She cannot give birth unless she brings her children to baptism, that is, unless she has the ability to evangelize. The catholicity of the Church is strictly concomitant with her ability to make disciples, evangelize, and baptize.

The Oneness of the Church

Every individual can unite with the person of Christ, becoming one with Him. However, we cannot unite with the Church unless we unite with her living members. Union with the Church necessitates the acceptance of a living membership in her body, a membership requiring a unity of members. Accordingly, members of the Church become one harmonious unit. Therefore, the catholicity of the Church is in her oneness, a perfect and complete oneness, not in terms of her structure, title, or any sterile quality, but in terms of the efficacy of her essence; that is, the ability of her body to unify. The nature of the Church is, in fact, like the nature of Christ: she is able to make the two one (cf. Eph. 2:15). Those who are unalike she forms into the same likeness—that of Christ.

The Church is "catholic," but her catholicity is in the oneness of her living body, a oneness which is unparalleled among human societies.

The Person is a Living Unit in the Church

At the same time, we find that every person of us is a living unit within the Church. We retain our own freedom, unique personality, features and independent existence. We are not merely cells in a body or building blocks in a social structure. Therefore, the Church is considered a unique personality in her kind: each member in her is, in fact, a church, and the Church altogether is Christ in His body and person.

If we fathom the depths of the mystery of the Church in the Spirit—as it will be revealed one day—we will find that she is the greatest human society that ever existed. In her uniqueness—that is, in her living body—she encompasses the greatest number of people, a multitude beyond what the mind can conceive. She embraces all peoples and races, all cultural customs, in one cooperative, symphonic unity among members who, despite being utterly dissimilar, work together in harmony (cf. 1 Cor. 12:4-30).

By and large, if we fathom the depth of the Church, we conclude that when the Church is perfected and manifested in her glory and splendor, we will see in her the true humanity, the humanity as God intended to create it. Until now, humanity has failed to fulfill God's purpose. So, God allowed us to disintegrate into myriads of human entities. Yet he intends for people to make a perfect human being according to His purpose. This is the Church! She is the body of Christ, in which Christ will be the head of that one human being.

CHAPTER TWO

THE CHURCH TRANSCENDS
SUFFERING

Suffering leads to self-actualization, though at the time it may seem to hinder the fulfillment of self-demands. However, the moment we joyfully embrace suffering, it transforms into the most compelling evidence of our self-actualization.

Feeling pain is a sign of life. Is not pain the experience of a living person, not the dead? Whenever we suffer, we manifest the depths of life in us.

Whenever we endure the test of suffering, we reveal the strength and firmness of the life we live.

Whenever we joyfully endure pain, we reveal another life better than the life of suffering we live on earth. Whenever we endure suffering, it clearly reveals that we live in the fullness of the better life (cf. Heb. 11:35; John 10:10).

If suffering leads to death for our witness to Jesus and the word of God, we will have fought the good fight that leads to the resurrection of eternal life (cf. Rev. 20:4). The Church lives in the deepest recesses of the better life. The majority of her members are now living in eternal life because they have fought the good fight, bearing their sufferings and torments in their bodies, which are the marks of the Lord Jesus (cf. Gal. 6:17). Their testimony is still alive and emanates from the graves of the martyrs and the hearts of those who are captives of hope, forever and ever.

Suffering as One of the Goals of the Church

The Spirit of the Church does not die away by persecution, and her character is not weakened by suffering, for her Spirit is divine and her personality possesses the features of the Lord Jesus. Do not think that suffering was brought on the Church as a secondary, additional work. Christ did not suffer as something supplementary but rather, suffering was the ultimate purpose of the incarnation (cf. John 18:11) and the primary goal for which the Son of God descended was to fulfill it. On the cross Christ declared "it is finished" (John 19:30).

Likewise, the Church, which is Christ's body, must fill up what is lacking in the afflictions of Christ in her flesh—that is, her faithful members—for the sake of His body (cf. Col. 1:24). This is what the Apostle Paul declared about himself as a member of the Church and as a model for the rest of the members, that is, for the Church, by saying, "I fill up in my flesh what is lacking in the afflictions of Christ ,for the sake of His body, which is the Church" (Col. 1:24).

Therefore, the Church does not view suffering as an act alien to her body, trembling from it, or as a heavy yoke that she avoids. On the contrary, the Apostle James expresses with his words the Church's thought by saying, "Count it all joy when you fall into various trials" (Jas. 1:2). She is not crushed by suffering, nor is she overwhelmed by it. Instead, the Church elevates and transcends it, carrying it in her body as an ornament and placing it on her head as a crown. Is the cross not her pride (cf. Gal 6:14)?

Suffering is a testimony. It represents for the Church what it is for Christ: it reveals the mystery of life hidden behind the cross and bears witness to love and sacrifice. It is not possible to proclaim the Christian life if we hide from suffering because suffering, as we said, is an attribute of the living, not the dead.

Suffering as a Sign of the Healing of the Member in the Suffering Body of Christ

If the endurance of suffering is considered a point of strength by psychologists because it indicates a strong will and persistence, in the Christian life it is considered a grace (cf. 1 Pet. 2:20). If a member endures suffering and participates in it with the Church by carrying her yoke and advocating for her, it is considered a sure sign of his or her connection to the body of Christ.

How awesome is the grace and great is the gift to be suffering members of Christ's Church! "For to you it has been granted on behalf of Christ, not only to believe in Him, but also to suffer for His sake" (Phil. 1:29). If participating in the Church's joy, celebrations, and feasts brings spiritual pleasure, then sharing in her sufferings, distresses, and persecutions should be considered a sign of a member's health. It is a sign that the Church's spirit flows in them.

Attending church and participating in her mysteries qualify us for union with Christ. However, the sign of our unity with other members, and even with the Head Himself—Christ—will be bearing the yoke of suffering in the church, enduring hardships and persecutions for the sake of the Word, and sharing in the needs of the weak and sick. It is a true unity in which the Spirit of the Church flows in us to fill us with faith, truth, knowledge, zeal, and love. Then the spirits of the martyrs and saints dwell in us, and their power rests upon us just as the spirit of Elijah rested on Elisha and John the Baptist.

Therefore, the Church prays at the end of the offering of incense, when the priest invokes the blessings of the Virgin Mary, the angels, the martyrs, the apostles, the saints, and all the righteous of the Church, saying:

> May their holy blessing, their grace, their power, their gift, their love, and their help be with us all, forever. Amen.[1]

This supplication does not sound strange to us. Aren't we all living members with them and united in one body?

The Need and Honor of Suffering with the Church

Thus, we can understand the extent of our intense need to interact with this body, i.e., the members of the Church. What honor and dignity we receive when we unite with this body, becoming one, not only with its saints but even more so with its poor, needy, suffering, and persecuted members. For these saints became holy only because they were also poor, needy, suffering, and persecuted (cf. Heb. 11:36-37).

Christ refers to the hungry, the thirsty, the strangers, the naked, the sick, and the imprisoned as His brethren (cf. Matt. 25:40). He further elevates them by identifying them

---

[1] The Divine Liturgies of Saints Basil, Gregory and Cyril (Los Angeles, 2001):66.

as His own person, He does not say they are the "likeness of His person" but as "His very person," that is His body we are talking about ,which is the Church .The Lord said: "Assuredly, I say to you, inasmuch as you did it to one of the least of these My brethren, you did it to Me" (Matt. 25:40). The Lord does not only call our attention to the act of giving, but rather He wants us to appreciate and honor those to whom we minister with the same reverence we offer to the person of Christ. He then elevates us at the end of His discourse in Matt. 25:40 to introduce us into the presence of the wondrous mystery in which He reveals that the least of His brethren—the hungry, thirsty, strange, homeless, naked, sick, imprisoned bodies—are His own mystical body, i.e., the Church.

It is evident, then, that our vitality in the body of Christ depends on our response to bear our urgent share in the needs of the weak, sick, and suffering members.

Suffering as a Passport to Glory

Although the Church seems to be suffering outwardly, in reality, her sufferings should be considered the price of her glory. Many members have been drawn to the church by her appearance, and were happy to work and labor for her by ministering and preaching, among other things. However, when they discovered her reality and the cost of glory, i.e., suffering, they collided with it and were shocked.

They started circling around her, avoiding entry into her divine sphere. They avoided suffering by means of hypocrisy and adulation. They got rid of persecution through flattery and affectation, skirting around the truth, for they considered their lives more valuable to them than the Cross. They used earthly wisdom to discern reality; they thought they could please God and people at the same time, or come to terms with the rulers of this age without relinquishing the kingdom of God. They easily "falter between two opinions" (1 Kgs. 18:21) and achieve notable success in the eyes of the worldly populace. However, although they minister to the Church, they are not members of her living body. They may be scholars or preachers, but they are not counted among her saints.

Present Sufferings are the Sap of Eternal Life

The significance of suffering and the persecution in which the Church lives without ceasing is revealed before us. Persecutions and tribulations are not only a test for the members but also the sap of life through which the Church's body grows. If the branches of the vine accept the sap of life, its life will flow in them, so they become firm, rooted, and fruitful. However, suppose the branches recoil and refuse such a sap. In this case, they dry up and wither away, for suffering is a cardinal element in the Church's very being; she rises through it and eventually above it.

Many have persecuted her in secret and in public; some of them were her sworn enemies, and some were her own children. The latter were pushed by the Evil One and the adversary of good, who hardened their hearts. However, they never knew they were working for the devil's sake and toward their own perdition. Little did they realize that by persecuting others, they were unwittingly forging crowns of martyrdom for the persecuted members. Times of persecution are times of revival of love and growing.

The Church remains the Church; she is an ever-growing

entity. Despite all that has been done to her in the past and that will be done in the future, the elect continue to join her. Her living sphere becomes more vibrant as a result of her suffering. During such times of adversity, the love of her active members is rekindled, and she thrives. She gains new members attracted by the desire for sacrifice and enthralled by the splendor of martyrdom for the Truth.

The Scene of Golgotha is Renewed Every Day

The Church is perpetually crucified, and her betrayers are her own children. On the one hand, she always resides among crucifying members and, on the other, remains among loving, selfless members. She is surrounded by a blaspheming thief on her left and a glorified, repentant thief confessing his sins on her right. Around her are false witnesses, but within her are also honorable fathers and mothers, confessors of faith. She contains both wolves and sheep, both wheat and tares. She will, however, arise when her bridegroom arrives, and cut off the false members of her body. The Church militant and the saints will then be raptured with those who have fallen asleep so that they all may be together as righteous and perfect ,accompanied by thousands of thousands of angels in a festal gathering.

Some False Personalities Inside the Church

Inside the Church, we are faced by those who are accused of straining out the gnat, and those who cling to the horns of the altar (cf. Matt. 23:24; 1 Kgs. 1:51).

The Church always lives having within her members who merely possess the appearance of godliness (cf. 2 Tim. 3:5): they cling to postures, forms, and words, meticulously straining out the gnat (cf. Matt. 23:24), and washing the cup from the outside (cf. Matt. 23:25). They do this to show off their cleanness before the people, crying out: "The temple of the Lord, the temple of the Lord, the temple of the Lord" (Jer. 7:4) in the language of their ancestors who killed the prophets (cf. Matt. 23:31). They try to influence the naive (cf. Rom. 16:18) in their actions, with the result that, eventually, they end up swallowing the camel and neglecting justice and mercy (cf. Matt. 23:23-24).

We also find those who work and exert themselves for their own benefit. The Church encompasses members who toil and labor, or appear to do so, as if nothing existed in their lives besides the Church. However, their toil and labor accrue solely to their own benefit (Rom. 16:18); the Church derives nothing from them. These are transient members whom the Church will dismiss when the bridegroom arrives.

However, the Church has members who are unknown—wealthy or impoverished, wise or naive, adults or children, young men or women—who not only have the form of godliness but also possess its power in their inner lives as a mystery. No one recognizes them to praise them, and they do not display a false godliness in order to receive praise. Their knowledge and education are not noticeable to be praised on the pulpits. Their prayers are performed in secret, and if they are performed in public, they are not ostentatious. They do not linger in their prayers, and they do not blow a trumpet before them, so they do not attract much attention. These are the Church's living body. Nonetheless, they are not immune to suffering.

There are also those in the Church who, due to their talents, cannot be tolerated by any place or leader. In fact, their spiritual gifts do not help them resist, as they are gifts of meekness and humility, which cannot be used as weapons. These persons are humiliated, live as sojourners, and preach in their exiles wherever they are scattered.

Their persecutors never cease to persecute them, and yet these meek persons never cease to serve their Master. Persecutors fabricate false accusations and testimonies against them to conceal the scandal of their oppression, justify their persecution, relieve their conscience's torment, or appear innocent before the public. However, the truth cannot remain concealed forever. Whether the persecuted are alive or dead, whether they desire it or not, the word of truth that is in their hearts and mouths must one day be revealed.

Mordecai cannot be crucified on the cross set up for him, because Haman has in fact set up the cross for himself (cf. Esther 7). And after the sentence of oppressors, comes that of history, and after the judgment of people, comes that of the heavenly court.

And the cross of Christ is still terrifying and bitter to Annas and Caiaphas.

The Church will adorn and perfume herself with the suffering members of the Church's body on the day she is summoned to meet the Lord, because they exude the scent of Golgotha.

CHAPTER THREE

THE CHURCH TRANSCENDS
SECTARIANISM

It pains us to hear the prophecy fulfilled at the Cross: "For My clothing they cast lots" (Ps. 22:18; John 19:24). Could anyone fathom that such a lot would be cast among the disciples on Christ's body? That these disputants would tear it asunder, distributing its pieces so that each disciple might claim what the outcome of the lot held for them? But praise be to God that they did not do that; they were unable to do so, because "not a bone of Him shall be broken" (John 19:36; Ps. 34:20).

How, then, do we dare do this in such a shameless manner? Without even drawing lots, we tear, or rather attempt to tear, this Body with strivings, schisms, heresies, and numerous sects. "Is Christ divided?" (1 Cor. 1:13). But praise be to God that the body of Christ is indivisible and cannot be torn asunder. The true Church of Christ transcends sectarianism, schisms, heresies, and denominations, standing firm above time and suffering like a mountain. Not only by her unwavering orthodoxy and belief in salvation, but rather, by her members who believed in her, and have been saved. They stand as witnesses to her in heaven, not as if they had lived in her past and vanished, but as living members in her present, constituting her heavenly temple, working and praying for our sake so that we can fulfill their likeness (cf. Heb. 11:40).

The Church is a tremendous force comprising countless saints who have completed their race, battle, and service on earth, and are still ministering to those on earth from heaven (cf. Rom. 5:11). As for those who created schisms within the Church and unjustly showed her hostility, they are deceivers; they acquired her faith and love, yet, they stepped out of her and adorned themselves with different strange names, despite the fact that Orthodoxy remains at the core of their faith and salvation, regardless of how they alter their appearance. Is the creed of Saint Athanasius not their creed? Is not their Christianity the result of seeds sown long ago in her land, and watered by the blood of her martyrs?

Does a child forget his mother if he is temporarily separated from her? He will inevitably love her again, and even if he did not truly know her, he will learn to love her when he returns. Was not this the story of Oedipus?[1] In the spirit of prophecy, Isaiah said this about the Church in her final days: "For as a young man marries a virgin, so shall your sons marry you" (Isa. 62:5). Consider the spirit of prophecy: how does a son marry his mother unless he abandons her in stubbornness and ignorance of his sonship for many days, then returns to her not knowing her, and finally marries her

---

[1] Oedipus, a king of Thebes in Greek mythology, is a tragic hero who unwittingly fulfils a prophecy that foretold he would kill his father and marry his mother, resulting in catastrophe for his city and family (translators' note).

when he loves her? When shall our mother-bride adorn herself and wear her splendid dress so that her children may return to her? When shall we unveil the truth that is in her, so that our brothers and sisters who left us in their stubbornness may return to us to live in the communion of love? Such brethren will surely return with many spoils: souls from Africa, Asia, Europe, and the islands of distant seas.

Lift up your eyes all around, and see: They all gather together, they come to you; Your sons shall come from afar, and your daughters shall be nursed at your side. Then you shall see and become radiant, and your heart shall swell with joy; Because the abundance of the sea shall be turned to you, the wealth of the Gentiles shall come to you (Is. 60:4-5).

It is then that her name, chosen in the spirit of prophecy, will be fulfilled: "One, Only, Holy, Catholic, and Apostolic Church."

Sectarianism does not hinder the catholicity of love. Let us not be puffed up as if true faith were our monopoly; a simple loving glance at our brethren who are separated from us would compensate for the lethal sectarianism that characterizes our Christianity.

When we hate and persecute those who do not share our faith, we commit heinous crimes and sins in the name of our credos of faith. Do credos of truth breed hatred? Do the tenets of the Orthodox faith breed animosity? Does the commandment of love inspire persecution?

Let us hear the counsel of St. James the venerable Apostle: "Out of the same mouth proceed blessing and cursing. My brethren, these things ought not to be so. Does a spring send forth fresh water and bitter from the same opening? "(Jas. 3:10-11).

You might protest by saying, "They are the ones who slander and hate." But I will reply, "This may befit the son who is separated from his mother, but not the Church who is the Mother of all. You are a representative of this Mother who endures the harassment of her son, because she hopes and even trusts that he will return.

Yet, catholicity of love does not justify hypocrisy and faltering. Friendship, love, and cordiality should not lead us to relinquish or compromise the principles of our faith, for faith in Christ is valued with the blood of thousands of martyrs, handed down to us by the apostles through generations upon generations. Also, we should not undervalue or compromise our dogmatic and spiritual heritage and the traditions of our worship that are the image of our Mother. Her form will one day attract her offspring if we fully comprehend it. On one hand ,let us not treat our heritage as if it were of little value; on the other hand, let us not blindly cling to it, otherwise we may face criticism and that will lead to our collapse. It is pointless to defend this spiritual heritage if we have not personally experienced and tasted it in our lives. Otherwise, this fertile heritage will shrivel and die, no matter how hard we try to protect it with our pens and words.

Our Heritage is a Living Part of Our Being

This heritage has been imprinted on the nature of successive generations, as a component of our moral behavior, as a characteristic of our intellectual ideals, and as a source of our psychological tendencies, whether in individuals, families, or groups. It is the outward manifestation of our understanding of Christ's essence and the gospel's truth. Therefore, it is a theological legacy.

Any attempt to undermine this pervasive heritage risks destabilizing the foundations of faith and life in general. And any attempt to do so will result in dire consequences, as was the case in those countries that rejected their heritage and changed, creating their own cultures in accordance with psychological and educational theories. Such nations are currently in a state of grave moral decay, in which the faith's foundations have been irreparably shaken, and they are plagued by terrible intellectual and spiritual setbacks. These states of moral decay began with small movements toward revising the ancient heritage.

The true unity of the Church of Christ cannot be realized only by ecumenical dialogues and interchurch councils with their endless decisions and recommendations.[2] There is an immediate need for a sound re-evangelization and a genuine call to renew the lives of individuals and nations before the believers can be united or the faith can be unified. The day we come to Christ with a sincere heart and experience the reality of our salvation, we will all inevitably join together in one spiritual Church.

---

[2] See Matthew the Poor, *The Mystery of Unity* (St. Macarius Press: Wadi al-Natrun, 2024; translators' note)

CHAPTER FOUR

TEACHING
AND FATHERHOOD
INSIDE THE CHURCH

Teaching in the Church

"Teacher" was the most common and cherished and beloved title of the Lord Jesus (cf. John 13:13). Although people may have a multitude of teachers, there is only one true Teacher for the entire world: the Lord Jesus Christ (cf. Matt. 23:10). This is because His teaching is the personal teaching of God. As Jesus stated explicitly in John's Gospel:

> My teaching is not mine, but his who sent me. If anyone's will is to do God's will, he will know whether the teaching is from God or whether I am speaking on my own authority (John 7:16-17 ESV).

This is the criterion of the true teaching, and of *the* teacher of Truth: that the teacher is sent from God, and that His teaching is for the glory of the One who sent Him,

He who speaks from himself seeks his own glory; but He who seeks the glory of the One who sent Him is true, and no unrighteousness is in Him (John 7:18).

Therefore, anyone who dares to teach in the name of God without being sent by Him should not be considered a teacher; he speaks from himself and seeks his own glory. He is a usurper because he embezzles God's glory for himself.

Philosophers' Logic

The term "teacher" carries great and outstanding connotations because it denotes an individual who speaks from his own knowledge, not acquired from others. Philosophers and sages reasoned in this manner. As a result, each philosopher was often called a "teacher" because of his own original, unprecedented school of thought. His disciples relied on his authority and teachings.

If we apply the above criterion to one who speaks or preaches about Christ, we must only refer to him as a "disciple." Regarding human logic and philosophical conventions, he does not qualify as a "teacher." If he deserves the title "disciple," it is already a great honor, and it is sufficient to refer to him as such because he is merely a transmitter of the mind of Christ (cf. Matt. 10:25).

Christ's Logic

What was just described is the logic of philosophers and man, not the logic of Christ. Christianity is not a branch of human sciences, but a divine truth that people cannot learn on their own. Neither can the human mind comprehend Christ's logic, regardless of how wise or well-versed in philosophy one may be. To understand what Christianity is about, we must possess the Spirit of Christ: "Now if anyone does not have the Spirit of Christ, he is not His" (Rom. 8:9). In addition, we must change and renew our minds until we are worthy of Christ's thought: "For who has known the mind of the Lord that he may instruct Him? But we have the mind of Christ." (1 Cor. 2:16). Moreover, we must eat the Body and Blood of Christ, and be united to Him through faith for Christ to dwell in us with His living person: "...that Christ may dwell in your hearts through faith" (Eph. 3:17).

Thus, this is what one must do to know Christ and the revealed truth of Christianity. Those who wish to teach about Christ or Christianity must also possess a unique talent: "The word of knowledge through the same Spirit" 1) Cor. 12:8).

If we wish to preach Christ to others, we must do so through Christ, i.e., Christ must dwell in us with His very person and preferred title, "Teacher." In doing so, we will preach Christ through Christ. It will not be us who preach, but rather, "the Spirit of our Father who speaks in us" (cf. Matt. 10:20). Moreover, we must refrain from speaking on our own and should say nothing except what God gives us: "For I will give you a mouth and wisdom which all your adversaries will not be able to contradict or resist" (Luke 21:15).

Whoever has Christ has in himself *the* "Teacher" (cf. 2 Cor. 13:3). And so, preaching through the mouth of Christ, uttering words by the Holy Spirit, and teaching the personal knowledge of Christ (not "about" Christ but through Christ), he is henceforth no longer a disciple but the beloved Teacher of Galilee, Nazareth, and Capernaum Himself, Who still teaches through us: "Teaching them to observe all things that I have commanded you; and lo, I am with you always, even to the end of the age" (Matt. 28:20).

Therefore, everyone whom God sent and gave the knowledge, truth, spirit, and mind of Christ and in whose heart Christ dwells through faith will be worthy to be called truly the "Teacher." For this person will not teach on his account or through himself, but by Christ; or rather, Christ teaches by him: "Now then, we are ambassadors for Christ, as though God were pleading through us: we implore you on Christ's behalf, be reconciled to God" (1 Cor. 5:10).

Thus, we are no longer many teachers: "My brethren, let not many of you become teachers" (Jas. 3:1). In fact, we are all the One "Teacher" because we preach with one Spirit, one Truth, one faith and one Lord, as we preach not ourselves or what is ours, but Christ teaches through us, for the Spirit "will take what is Mine and declare it to you" (John 16:14).

Christ the Teacher Sets Out the Characteristics of the "teacher"

Christ was the Teacher par excellence, set before us as a model for mankind. Christ Himself said that He never spoke on His own, but that all He said He first heard from His Father (cf. John 8:26,28,38). Neither did He ever do anything of His own accord, but only what His Father wanted Him to (cf. John 10:37). Nor did He ever will anything other than what was in accordance with His Father (cf. John 4:34; 5:30). Not that He lacked the knowledge or independent will to do so, but He "emptied Himself" (Phil. 2:7) of all that belonged to Him in order to receive the work of His Father and thus fulfill in a most amazing way the meaning of obedience and submission.

146

All this is evident, even though He is the one who said: "All that the Father has is Mine" (John 16:15 ;("All Mine are Yours" (John 17:10); "I and My Father are one" (John 10:30). He was drawing our attention to the fact that the Son is never lacking in anything with respect to the Father; the Son is equal to the Father in everything. Yet, the Son *emptied* Himself of everything that belonged to Him in order to think, act, and will through the Father only, and not by His own direction. He thus perfected the law of obedience and submission to give us the perfect and precise model, and the mystical means by which we can accept God's thought, work, and will in us.

Thus, as we acquire Christ in us, we can be like Him, easily *emptying* ourselves by His grace from everything that is ours, whether it be private knowledge, personal occupations, or self-will, so that God's will, knowledge, and action may dwell in us.

It is only then that we can understand the Lord's saying, "Do not be called teachers; for One is your Teacher, the Christ" (Matt. 23:10). In other words, it is not a matter of personal titles, for there will never be anyone except the One "Teacher."

Only the Church Confers the Title of "Teacher"

From whom can we derive the spirit, mind, truth, or knowledge of Christ that we may preach Christianity? Or, in other words, upon what shall we draw to acquire the person of Christ so that we may preach Him? There must be one source from which to draw all that belongs to Christ in order to learn the same teaching and become the same teacher. Such a source should not include any schism, divergence, or conflicting views; otherwise, we would not be able to preach the same teaching or become all one master (cf. 1 Cor. 1:10–13).

Where else can we obtain this outside the Church, the body and bride of Christ from Whom we receive the mystery of renewal, the communion of the Spirit, the knowledge of the gospel, and the truth? We receive Christ in His living person from the Church when He is revealed to us through her mysteries. Therefore, we accept Him through faith, and He dwells in our hearts with His unique Person, the beloved Teacher of Capernaum.

Qualifications of the Church as the Bestower of the Title of "Teacher"

The Church possesses the mind, truth, and knowledge of Christ, not only in her scriptures, books, and commentaries; but also in her members, the disciples, who witnessed the Lord Jesus, lived with Him, and received the Tradition from Him. In addition, there are those to whom He revealed Himself after His Ascension, who heard His voice from heaven, and understood His will.

> The God of our fathers has chosen you that you should know His will, and see the Just One, and hear the voice of His mouth. For you will be His witness to all men of what you have seen and heard (Acts 22:14-15).

All of these disciples and apostles are living members with us in the body of the Church, given to us to be united with. We have a communion with them through the Church, and their spirit bolsters us and reveals to us the mystery of the truth and the knowledge that is treasured in Christ.

To me, who am less than the least of all the saints, this grace was given, that I should preach among the Gentiles the unsearchable riches of Christ, and to make all see what is the fellowship of the mystery, which from the beginning of the ages has been hidden in God who created all things through Jesus Christ; to the intent that now the manifold wisdom of God might be made known by the church to the principalities and powers in the heavenly places (Eph. 3:8-10).

Therefore, the Church possesses the mystery of teaching that the members receive from her, just as they receive life, spirit, and renewal. Thus, the truth hidden to many is revealed: that the Church is the one constant source of teaching because she gives everything that belongs to Christ, and indeed even Christ Himself. The character of the Church bears the title of the immortal Christ, the "Teacher."

It is, therefore, unlawful for anyone who is not a living member of the Church body to use the title "teacher" and assume the function of a "teacher," that is, the pastor. He must have received the mystery or gift of teaching and shown the signs of the mission, which is to proclaim Christ's truth and His thought, and to have the Word alive in his mouth and heart. The Holy Spirit dwelling within him will give him what belongs to Christ, speaking through him to reconcile all people to God.

False Titles

People bestow many titles upon one another in the Church that are not in accordance with Christ's truth, nor do their bearers show the signs and power of His mission. In this case, they are nothing but false titles, and the Church recognizes neither them nor their bearers.

Moreover, according to Christ, anyone who dares sit on the chair of teaching in the Church while unqualified as a "teacher," or still in the penitent phase, is alien to the body of the Church, and a usurper as Christ said, "He who speaks from himself seeks his own glory; but He who seeks the glory of the One who sent Him is true, and no unrighteousness is in Him" (John 7:18).

Fatherhood in the Church

Good is the Lord's saying: "Do not call anyone on earth your father; for One is your Father, He who is in heaven" (Matt. 23:9). Who is the true Father if not the one who redeems His children with His own life, even to the point of death? Though we can see a faint miniature of fatherhood in earthly life typified by a father's love for his children, yet it is an incomplete picture, for it is possible that a father may neglect his own children, or abandon them for God's sake and in order to minister to other children of God.

However, we see true fatherhood shining brightly in God's fatherhood for us, as He gave Himself to us in His Son, even to His death on the cross. He redeemed us from death to live for Him.

Christ Hands Down to us the Spirit of Fatherhood

Jesus sacrificed Himself, endured suffering, and submitted to death on the cross in order to redeem us from death and bring us before His Father alive and blameless. In this way, He demonstrated to us the spirit of true fatherhood. He then gave us His body, blood, and Spirit so that we might have a taste of this fatherhood, with the same spirit of sacrifice and the same intensity of love that can make us fathers. In this fatherhood we may also endure suffering to the point of death for others' sake, just as He did for our sake.

Such is the genuine and authentic nature of fatherhood. Thus, in Christ, we have the potential for fatherhood, not because of our own will or piety but because of the power of the One who died and rose for our sake.

Therefore, the sign of genuine, unadulterated fatherhood is the presence of Christ within us; that is, our willingness to sacrifice. The evidence of His death is visible in us as we endure His sufferings and the bitterness of His cup: "From now on let no one trouble me, for I bear in my body the marks of the Lord Jesus" (Gal. 6:17).

These are the signs of fatherhood: those who wish to become fathers should not hold their lives dear, nor should they consider themselves to be something of significance. They should be able to lay down their lives joyfully through the power of Christ in them for the salvation of others; not out of personal valor, boasting, or even a sense of having done their children a great favor, but out of the tenderness of fatherhood. They should be completely oblivious to their own possessions and remember only the need of others for salvation through love, in accordance with the Spirit of Christ within them.

So, affectionately longing for you, we were well pleased to impart to you not only the gospel of God, but also our own lives, because you had become dear to us... As you know how we exhorted, and comforted, and charged every one of you, as a father does his own children (1 Thess. 2:8-11).

We should not be surprised by such words, because it is not Paul who speaks, suffers, and is willing to spend and be spent for them (cf. 2 Cor. 12:15), but it is Christ in Paul (cf. Gal. 2:20). According to Paul's own words, "Paul" knows how "Saul" used to persecute the Church of God, tried to destroy it beyond measure, and conducted himself in the lusts of his flesh just as the others (cf. Eph. 2:3).

The Spirit of Christ makes the wolf a sheep, and the sheep a shepherd. Paul, the lion that used to breathe threats and murder (cf. Acts 9:1), turned into a meek lamb. The stray and rebellious son became a merciful father because the blood of the Lamb was sprinkled upon him; Paul received the effect of the spirit of blood and life in which dwells the power of love. This power was kindled in his heart for the sake of others.

Thus, Paul and every person in Christ Jesus become merciful fathers, not having the arrogance of false fatherhood but the kindness, tenderness, mercy, and compassion of our Lord Jesus.

> But we were gentle among you, just as a nursing mother cherishes her own children. So, affectionately longing for you, we were well pleased to impart to you not only the gospel of God, but also our own lives, because you had become dear to us (1 Thess. 2:7-8).

Surely, such a person has the right to bear the title of fatherhood because he bears the tender mercies of Christ towards his children, and such a father has the right to be proud of his children: "Therefore, my beloved and longed-for brethren ,my joy and crown" (Phil. 4:1). He even has the right to confidently boast of his fatherhood in Christ, because he has begotten them for Christ:

> For though you might have ten thousand instructors in Christ, yet you do not have many fathers; for in Christ Jesus I have be-

gotten you through the gospel (1 Cor. 4:15).

Fatherhood is Vigilance, Tears, and Teaching

Fatherhood such as this is not a title, occupation, or trade; rather, it entails sufferings, tears, sleeplessness, toil and labor in compassion, teaching, preaching, and setting a virtuous example.

Paul labored in the womb of his fatherhood to give birth to his children until Christ was formed in them (cf. Gal. 4:19). Thus, after being enslaved by uncleanness they were born to him as God's children. In fact, the Apostle Paul left us a full-fledged fatherly inheritance. He did so by immortalizing the value of celibacy in fatherhood so that natural fatherhood would not contend with spiritual fatherhood, and so that the children of a slave woman, or of the flesh, would not look down on the children of a free woman or of the Spirit (cf. Gal. 4:23.29). This is also demonstrated by the fact that he abandoned his family and clan in Tarsus, never mentioning them in any of his letters, so that he could devote himself entirely to his fatherly work within the family of Christ, serving the saints and the people of God's house.

He viewed the warmth of his family as 'rubbish' (cf. Phil. 3:8), and the affection of his relatives as an impediment to the mission (cf. Luke 9:62). In addition, this Pauline heritage can also be observed in his sojourning without having a stable city or abode. In contrast with his early family life in Tarsus, after he came to know Christ, his life was spent in permanent exile, wandering for the sake of the gospel (cf. 1 Cor. 4:11).

Paul bore slandering, calumny, ridicule, betrayal, and opposition either from his fellow country people, or from the class of Roman rulers, Greek scholars, and his own traitorous children. They turned away from him and opposed him, disregarding his fatherly sacrifices and his words of exhortation and education.

A Precious Heritage of a "Fatherhood that Became like a Flock"[1]

It was not only Paul who left us a legacy of fatherhood, now stored in the Church. Consider how John the Beloved, the celibate elder, was tortured in Patmos for being faithful to the fatherhood with which Christ entrusted him. Consider, as well, how all the disciples suffered and died to uphold the ties and responsibilities of fatherhood in the Church.

Behold Athanasius, Dioscorus, and Peter, "the seal of the martyrs," the founding fathers of Alexandria. Behold John Chrysostom, Severus, and other pillars of Constantinople and Antioch, and consider their mature fruitful fatherhood which bequeathed to the Church through their trust, sacrifice, sleeplessness, and teachings, whether in exile, flight, or stability.

What further shall I say? Time would run out if I listed each of the fruitful Church Fathers individually. Such fathers are comparable to fattened lamb sacrifices, emitting a sweet aroma similar to that of the cross. The Church adorned and perfumed herself with them in anticipation of the arrival of the Bridegroom.

---

[1] See Ps. 106:41 LXX "[He] makes fatherhood as a flock." This verse in the psalm denotes how fatherhood is transformed into a living sacrifice for the children (translators' note).

The Church Bears and Grants the Title of Fatherhood Deservedly

The Church carries the well-deserved title of fatherhood because she received it from the Spirit of the One Who died on the cross for the sake of His children. She bestows this title on anyone who resolves to die for Christ's sake and lay down his life for his beloved. Therefore, this person is referred to as "father" because he leads children to Christ, just as Christ led "many sons to glory" (Heb. 2:10).

But how can one be called a father in the Church, regardless of his position or name, if he is unwilling to lay down his life for others, fleeing not from a wolf or dog but from mere intimidation or threat?

Or how can he be called father in the Church if he is not ready to defend the right of Christ and his children at the expense of his comfort, honor, reputation, food, or job?

In addition, I ask: how is he called a father in the Church when he persecutes his children like a mother cat devouring her kittens after giving birth: slandering them, spreading false information about them, and initiating lawsuits and trials against them? How many courts have dealt with similar cases! (cf. Ezek. 34:4-5).

Or how can he be called a father in the Church if he is a temple thief robbing money from the altar, buying lands and real estate, or accumulating funds in banks?

If only these people knew that the Church is not an anonymous entity! Her Head in heaven, the Lord Jesus, sees, hears, and writes a book of remembrance.

It will be too bad when the truth is manifested at the coming of our Lord, the members of the Church are revealed, and we search for those whom we used to call our fathers, yet we may not find them in any part of the body of the Church.

Then we will see Lazarus with the group of the persecuted, who are humiliated and despised, standing with honorable members and crowned pillars in the Lord's temple, adorned not with medals or decorations but with the marks of the Lord Jesus.

The true Church is a congregation of holy fathers united not by titles but by their pain and suffering for the sake of the fatherhood entrusted to them in the Church, the body of Christ.

CHAPTER FIVE

THE CHURCH AND
THE HOLY SPIRIT

The Church began her work on the day of Pentecost by the action of the Holy Spirit displayed in power, fire, storm, and earthquake. This alerted the human senses to the work of the secret and invisible power that the Holy Spirit would perform to fulfill His mission in the temple of humanity. The effects of grace, wisdom, and strength that flew on the apostles and disciples brought about a reasoning which was uncontradictable and irresistible. The signs and miracles that followed them were a clear testimony that man had indisputably acquired the Spirit of God into his nature.

The event of the Pentecost was not one of the fruits of the Spirit, but it was one of His divine effects in man. To this day, the Spirit is not restrained from man, nor has it stopped or diminished, as man acquired Him in his dead nature as a Spirit of eternal life, to complement His work for the new creation of man in Christ Jesus. Through the Spirit, man could live in the Kingdom of God.

However, the action of the Holy Spirit in man was not without revelation or apparent embodiment. The nature of the Spirit was clearly revealed and overtly embodied in the writings of the apostles and disciples; that is, the Gospels and the epistles, in words which were "spirit and life" (cf. John 6:63).

The Holy Spirit was not content with the written word to reveal His nature, but He took His course into the nature of man directly by means other than the word—yet, through it—that is, in the mysteries He established in the Church. Through them, the flow of the Holy Spirit has not been interrupted in the Church until this hour.

If we are granted a revelation of the nature of the Holy Spirit in the Scriptures, through which we discover love and know the Truth, then in the mysteries we are granted the work of this same nature; we receive its permanent action in our nature, so we are united with the Truth and live it out.

After that, it is truly astonishing and sad to hear people asking for the coming of the Holy Spirit, as on the day of Pentecost. Is this not a blatant disregard for the truth of Pentecost, in which the Church lives, and a denial of the Holy Spirit's actual action in people?

The day of Pentecost, with all of the Spirit's power, action, and revealed nature, is always evident and present. Pentecost did not diminish, halt, or cease the work it began, and it will continue to fulfill it until man reaches "the stature of the fullness of Christ" (Eph. 4:13).

The gospel is the work of Pentecost and an overt revelation of the nature of the Holy Spirit. Has the gospel diminished or failed to reveal the nature of the Holy Spirit?

Here is the Church with her mysteries, in which the Holy Spirit is poured out, undergoing His action in us, so we receive the nature of the new creation in Christ Jesus. Did the mysteries fail to provide a path for the Holy Spirit into human nature? Is not the plea for a new Pentecost a blatant denial of the gospel already in your hands? Is it not a blasphemy against the action and power of mysteries? Is it not a sign of contempt toward the apostles and disciples, vessels chosen to carry the nature of the fiery spirit that was revealed in them through their words, deeds, knowledge, teaching and examples. Has time canceled their work? Or has the New Testament become so obsolete as to require a new Pentecost?

The descent of the Holy Spirit on the day of Pentecost necessitated vast changes in the entire human community. The chosen hearts of the apostles were prepared for these changes, having been appointed in the divine economy since eternity, before the creation of the world, and then having been trained by the Lord Himself for three years until they merited the acquisition of the fiery Spirit in them. The day of Pentecost is a single day in human history, but it was orchestrated so that humanity would be reborn in Christ. And indeed, it was reborn. It was the day human nature was betrothed to be a bride of Christ by the bond of the Holy Spirit. She was betrothed and married to Him forever.

Why then Pentecost? Pentecost was not an end in itself for the distribution of gifts to gladden and cheer the hearts of humanity. It was also not just a day for speaking new languages. Instead, it was an unprecedented day in human history that prepared human nature to receive and merit the nature of the Son of God, the Word.

Christ, as He was made known to us, is light, truth, and life. How then can we unite with light, truth, and life if we have a dark, ignorant and dead nature? How can we accept union with light if we are not endowed with the power of spiritual vision? How can we unite with the divine truth if we do not obtain the Spirit of truth? How can we be united with God's life without receiving the breath of God's Spirit in us?

For this reason, the Holy Spirit descended, and His nature was revealed in the word of the gospel so we may draw spiritual insight and knowledge of the truth from Him. Then, through the mysteries, He accomplished His work and action in us so we might receive the Spirit of life. For this reason, the Holy Spirit descended on Pentecost with a special power. This descent has never been and will never be repeated. The Holy Spirit is still at work in our nature to this day, through the gospel and the mysteries; therefore, a new Pentecost is not required. Rather, it is necessary to accept His work and action that He accomplished on the day of Pentecost and offered to us in the gospel and the holy mysteries.

Therefore, if we wish to be filled with the Spirit of Pentecost, we need to keep the commandments of Christ revealed in the gospel. We must completely submit our will and selves to the work of the Holy Spirit so that He may burn away from us everything that is not in accordance with Him and contrary to His will. Only then do we have the right to ask to be filled with the Spirit and to receive Him. To receive the fullness of the Pentecostal Spirit, which is present at all times in the gospel and in the mysteries, we must fulfill the requirements of Pentecost.

With the Spirit's two permanent loci of action, the gospel and the mysteries, the Church is immunized against the world. The world's evil operates in two arenas against man: the arenas of thought and spirit. In the first arena, that of thought, the Church is immunized by the word of the gospel, or rather by the Holy Spirit who is present and revealed as light and truth in Scripture. In the second arena, the arena of spirit, where Satan and his soldiers operate as evil, corrupting spirits in every corner of the earth and air, acting in the darkness, the Church has been immunized against them by the constant flow of the Holy Spirit through the mysteries.

Thus, Christ has not abandoned the Church as an orphan in the midst of a wicked world, but rather has immunized her against all errors.

Church's Infallibility

If we delve deeper into the nature of the Church, we will face the reality of her immunity from error, her infallibility.

The Church was first infallible in the persons of the apostles. The possibility of the apostles receiving the fiery nature of the Spirit was not an insignificant event. We cannot claim that the apostles received Him on their own worthiness or personal merit. But rather, it was Christ who freely sent the Holy Spirit, as He said: "For when the Helper comes, Whom I shall send to you from the Father" (John 15:26), "And I will pray the Father, and He will give you another Helper, that He may abide with you forever" (John 14:16).

However, we cannot overlook God's preparation for them to receive the Holy Spirit's fiery nature. The result of this preparation and the descent of the Holy Spirit in them as fire was the emergence of "the Church of the Apostles," as a human nature sanctified by the Holy Spirit.

This Church, sanctified by the Holy Spirit, was then qualified for an extraordinary divine work that required infallibility and transcending errors; namely, the recording of the words of the gospel as divine "spirit and life" written by the apostles while they were in a state of inerrancy.

In addition, the Church was prepared for another task that required the same level of transcendence over error; namely, the establishment of rituals perfectly suited to the Holy Spirit's indwelling and flow in her. So the mysteries were also established while the Church was in a state of inerrancy.

Therefore, we must comprehend the infallibility of the living Church as stemming from the word of the gospel and the power of the mysteries.

To remove the ambiguity around this brief definition, we should say that the word of the gospel is the Holy Spirit's nature as revealed to humankind and embodied in different writers, meaning that the word of the gospel is divine nature in human action. The gospel is not solely a divine work devoid of human impact. This divine nature has been received and then proclaimed by man. However, we are not talking about ordinary people here, but rather apostles and disciples.

Thus, the Church is the human nature that has been prepared to receive the nature of the Holy Spirit sent by the Father through the Son and by virtue of His merit, and which has earned the right to reveal the Holy Spirit's nature in the gospel and pave the way for His action in the mysteries. For this reason, it was necessary for the Church to be infallible in order to accomplish this divine mission.

In the same way that the Holy Spirit descended upon the body of the Virgin Mary to prepare her to receive the divine nature of the Son of God in her womb, the Holy Spirit descended upon the early Church to prepare her to acquire the divine nature of Christ and to receive the gospel and the mysteries.

After the Church was united with the divinity of the Son of God through the mediation of the Holy Spirit in both the gospel and the mysteries, the Church became not only human nature sanctified by the Holy Spirit, but also human nature united with Christ, the Son of God, by the sanctification of the Spirit through the gospel and the mysteries. In other words, the Church no longer only writes the gospel and receives the mysteries, but can also comprehend the gospel and administer the mysteries.

Is infallibility still valid today? Today, the reader's heart throbs with the question: Is the Church still infallible? To answer this question, we must first define the Church. Is the Church made up of her hierarchies and ministers? Or is it her teachings, words, and exegesis? Or does she consist of the biographies of her saints, whom she venerates with the utmost reverence? I think that it is not difficult for the reader now to perceive what the Church is, which we consider infallible. She is not the earthly flawed people, their words, or their lives. Rather, she is the human nature that was washed, sanctified, and justified in the name of the Lord Jesus and the Spirit of our God (cf. 1 Cor. 1:11), deemed worthy to receive the nature and the revelation of the Holy Spirit in the gospel, and its work in the mysteries, thus deserving to acquire the union with the nature of Christ, the Son of God.

Does the Church match this description, and do these details currently exist? Without a doubt, yes. Today's Church is the continuation of the divine incarnation and the indwelling of the Holy Spirit. She is made of our nature, and exists by our nature, and in our nature, possessing the power of the gospel, the mysteries, and the work of the nature of the Son of God.

She remains infallible and beyond the realm of error. She has never changed despite her leaders having changed; she has not been affected by the scandals and downfalls of her ministers, nor has she deviated from her unity despite the dreadful divisions that have occurred within her.

The word of truth in the Church is, in fact, firm and immutable, rooted in the gospel. And her access to the action of the Holy Spirit and the union with the Lord is also unchanged, existing as always in the mysteries.

Twenty centuries have passed, and only persons have changed in the Church. She is the same as she has been since day one: rooted in the gospel and alive in the mysteries. No sin can be found in her gospel, nor deceit in her mysteries.

It is not difficult now to comprehend the meaning, necessity, and limits of the term "infallibility." We can see infallibility as a divine state in which human nature is receptive to the fiery divine nature of the Holy Spirit. As for its necessity, the early Church, or rather the apostles, needed infallibility for two primary purposes: firstly, to totally accept the divine truth, uncontaminated by human thought, and its fixation through the writing of the gospel, letters, and the rest of the New Testament; secondly, establishing the Church's structure and mysteries on the foundation of the truth of the Scripture.

Regarding its limits, the infallibility is a divine state that the Church has acquired and will forever maintain. Infallibility removes human nature from the cycles of change, time, and space. Because of this, we observed that what the "infallible" Church has remained until now an unaltered truth, and what the apostles and disciples wrote in different places and at different times is one consistent truth.

The greater our comprehension of this truth, the better

we will be at avoiding errors. The more we cling to mysteries, the more infallible we become.

However, only the gospel and the mysteries will be absolutely infallible.

The Church that adheres to the gospel and the mysteries and comprehends and acts in accordance with them is in fact inside the realm of infallibility, and is spotless, and pure Church.

As long as patriarchs, bishops, priests, and people walk in holiness, they are infallible. As long as they adhere to the word of the gospel and receive the efficacy of the mysteries, they are free from error.

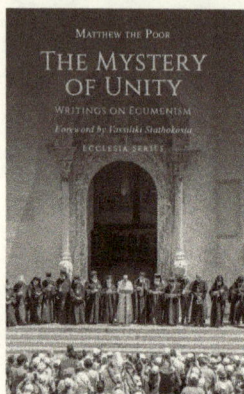